CARAVAGGIO AS A MODERNIST

CARAVAGGIO AS A MODERNIST
WHAT IS MODERNISM?

Dorit Kedar

Translated by
Irene Auerbach &
Raphael Kedar

THE CENTER OF INTERRELIGIOUS PEACE

CENTER OF INTERRELIGIOUS PEACE

The Center of Interreligious Peace
15 Oley Ha'Gardom St., Tel Aviv 6971523 ISRAEL

http://doritkedar.wordpress.com/

More titles by the author:
Cab Story, A Play
The Book of Interreligious Peace in Text and Image

Caravaggio as a Modernist: What is Modernism?

Original Hebrew title: *Caravaggio ke'modernist: mahu modernizem?*

Translation: Irit Auerbach, Raphael Kedar
Editor: Tzach Ben Josef
Initial editing: Raphael Kedar
Cover design and digital mastering: Gall Orian
Cover: *Head*, early 1990s, sculpture, mixed media, by the author
Photograph: Revital Topiol

© Dorit Kedar, The Center of Interreligious Peace, 2015

Bibliographic info: Kedar, Dorit. *Caravaggio as a Modernist: What is Modernism?* Tel Aviv: Center of Interreligious Peace, 2015.

ISBN 9789659214747

Printed by CreateSpace

To
My father, Salomon Shwartz and mother, Leontina Shwartz,
of blessed memory

My brethren and their spouses:
Raphael and Tamar Kedar
Daphna and Haim Kelman-Kedar
Gabriela and Amos Wolf-Kedar

Caravaggio
Sees the day
Lives at night
Pities the victim
Identifies with the killer
Enables light to be
And captures shadows.
In your manner, you have nurtured me
With poison
Till your complex image
Has been formed.

—DORIT KEDAR

CONTENTS

List of Illustrations

Measurements are given in centimeters

FOREWORD TO THE 2015 ENGLISH EDITION

This is not merely a book about Caravaggio; nor is it about Modernism. This is a book about everything that is in between: about what we think of when we say "Modernism" and about what we talk of when we think "Caravaggio." For these discourses and the book's main thesis—seeing in the modernist a reflection of a unique creative self and in consequence designating Caravaggio as such—to be truly brought to light, one must studiously venture off a well-beaten track of ostensible definitions and perceptions, both in art history and its philosophy, as well as in general patterns of thought.

This book is based on Dorit Kedar's 1988 MA thesis composed at the Art History Department of Tel Aviv University. Preceding this thesis were several seminars on Italian Mannerism. These attempted to demonstrate that the Mannerists sought an individual freedom of expression by deviating from traditional formal language, while still following the rigid rules of iconography. The Mannerist way of treating traditional art topics exposes the viewer to the possibility of perceiving the world of the unknown, of the enigma, of the mysterious, beyond time and space criteria, beyond the knowledge of men and women, beyond all dogma.

This open outlook continued to guide Kedar as she moved on to her MA thesis. It was further developed into a theoretical and empirical schema during her PhD studies in Creative Arts and

Eastern Philosophy at Union Institute and University in Ohio, culminating in her dissertation, "Zen Buddhism as Means to Increase Creativity." Zen Buddhism insights suggest a non-linear path in order to avoid the trap of subjective illusory reality and render possible the infinite spectrum of phenomena. All of the above projects and views eventually led to Kedar's monumental opus, *The Book of Interreligious Peace in Text and Image* (Tel Aviv: Center of Interreligious Peace, 2013). It aspires to expose the everlasting interlinks among all main beliefs and to widen paths of inclusion through feeling, towards a better grasp of the infinite, opening up channels which go beyond the cerebrally idiosyncratic.

With the completion and official publication of *The Book* in 2013, the road was fully paved to bring the current project—and others by the Center of Interreligious Peace—to the awareness of a larger international audience. In line with the Center's targets, the current project seeks to transmute traditional ways and methods of thought, and in the realm of the arts, to change the way these may be viewed, "read," and interpreted. In this regard, the golden rule of the current book's thesis is to locate in art such as Caravaggio's not another chain of antecedents that can be neatly placed one next to the other, but to fan out a wider array of links in intricate networks that go beyond chronology, period, style, etc. Accordingly, modernism is to be seen as more than a mere "term"—both in the sense of period and in having a precise definition. As such, this work has much to do with the innovative viewpoint and approach to art and art history evident in recent publications, like Alexander Nagel's *Medieval Modern: Art out of Time* (London: Thames and Hudson, 2012) or the latest keen interest in revisiting the texts of Warburg and Riegl.

The MA thesis was composed under the guidance of Profs. Gila Balas and Yona Pinson and was also evaluated by the then chair of the department, Prof. Nurith Kenaan-Kedar. Since then, it was adapted to a book in 2002 (in Hebrew; Tel Aviv: Hakibbutz Hameuchad). It has also been a required text in several art history courses and is widely circulated in major university libraries and in other establishments, in Israel and abroad.

Unlike its Hebrew counterpart, this book has been adapted relying on the entire written thesis of 1988. Nevertheless, it has been edited structurally and stylistically. In order to bring it up-to-date with current research and methodological approaches, the over-all structure of the original thesis was revised. In keeping with academic standards of scholarly work publishing, notes and references were reformatted and more images pertaining to the discussion added. Thus, the following is not a re-work or a re-issue altogether, as no additional data and analysis has been added to it, and nor has any information been added on the state of affairs regarding its subject-matter since its conception; that is, no attempt has been made to interpolate this work within recent or current scholarly work on either Caravaggio or Modernism.

In and on itself, this thesis is given ground by major scholars actively dealing with Modernism at the time of its composing, among others, John Russel, Linda Nochlin, Meyer Schapiro, and Herbert Read, and key Caravaggio scholars, mainly John Gash, Walter Friedlaender, and Howard Hibbard. As an adaptation of the MA thesis, therefore, it is within this milieu that the book should initially be considered since the breadth of writing on these matters has been vast since the 1980s.

All the same, though, this thesis can serve to reevaluate previous writings and to possibly re-examine the field of research on Caravaggio, as no scholar, best to my knowledge, has ever challenged to name Caravaggio a modernist in the unique way this book does. The modernist act in art is grasped as a manifestation of the artist's unique spirit and inner being not coinciding necessarily with that of his peers and the *zeitgeist*. Far exceeding, then, the range of an art-historical essay, this philosophical treatise on art, modernism, and individuality encourages a fresh outlook on situating the becoming of the work of art and its final analysis on several compatible lines.

These act as multiple entrance points for the discovery and comprehension of Caravaggio's art via issues that were not available or in their early stages of advancement when this thesis was being composed: matters of visual culture such as gender or queer theory, evident in Caravaggio's personal life which find their expression in his work (as in his androgynous Bacchus or his sexually-charged, boyish angels); ideas of performance—engagement on the part of the viewer with the work of art (for example, depicting the aggressor as victim and vice-versa, like his Judith or even the executioners in *Crucifixion of St. Peter*, where the viewers are encouraged to make up their own minds as to the nature of the acts being committed and their perpetrators); and even topics of phenomenology, anthropology of the image, and body studies, imminent in Caravaggio's images, which serve as a reflection of his exceptional mind and self-awareness, co-existing with his physical actions in the world evoking the formal aspects of his body of work (for instance, in his depiction of traditional themes, like saints; his St. Paul dumbfounded by the materialistically everyday darkness existentially surrounding him, being sprawled on the ground impotent after having being casually thrown off his horse, an act of mundane occurrence).

Attentive readers, then, shall notice—and benefit—from the unmediated observations prevalent in this book which establish a relationship between artist and reality, viewer and works of art. The true achievement of this book might be its directing the reader, viewer, and artist alike—of past, present, and even future—out towards a direct observance, which transcends norms, patterns, dogma, constraining theories, and pre-concepts of restricting time and space.

TZACH BEN JOSEF, EDITOR

ACKNOWLEDGMENTS

I would like to thank the people who have helped me along the way. For their involvement with the current English version I would like to thank the translator and editor of the Center of Interreligious Peace, Tzach Ben Josef, for editing, additional translating, and bringing this book up-to-date and to print. For the cover design, handling of images, and mastering of the digital version, the designer and digital master of the Center, Gall Orian. For his initial editing and translating, Raphael Kedar. Finally, a wholehearted show of gratitude to the translator and great friend, the late Irene Auerbach.

CARAVAGGIO AS A MODERNIST

INTRODUCTION

The title of this book requires a preliminary discussion of the term "Modernism." The basic question is whether it characterizes art only during the Modern Age, or, whether this term might be used to describe the characteristics of innovative original works of art in earlier periods. Within the context of this book, the term "modernism" is used as an indicator of quality, and not as an indicator of chronology, which pertains to the Modern Age. Thus, modernism is a way of creating, which is independent of the limitations of time, and relies upon the thought, spirit, and individuality of a particular creator. As an indicator of quality, not of chronology, it therefore, legitimizes the choice to accord a seventeenth-century artist the adjective modernist.[1]

John Russell characterizes modernism as the inner essence of the artist, asserting that modernism is not something that can be learned step-by-step, like bookkeeping. To come to terms with it means a many-years' struggle, in which faction is pitted against faction and the very basis of the enterprise is subject to calumny and recrimination.[2]

Contrary to Russell, Leopold Zahn attempts to analyze modernism on the basis of criteria that are both chronological and formal, such as color and treatment of the canvas surface. He does not take into consideration, however, the inner being of the artist but, rather, emphasizes external factors dependent on time and plastic effects.[3] Perhaps this is the reason why Zahn fails to reach a definitive conclusion concerning the meaning of modernism. Zahn is concerned with the external, while Russell prefers to address the artist's inner spirit and considers the work of art as a reflection of that unique spirit.

In Moshe Barasch's *Approaches to Art* one finds an intricate discussion concerning modernism based on Jacob Burckhardt's thesis. Burckhardt, like Russell, focuses on the artist's unique thought process and individuality rather than on his final product, the work of art.[4] In differentiating the classical from the modern, Burckhardt emphasizes two main characteristics: the first is that the content of "classic art" is conventional while "modern art" is a reflection of the artist's individuality. The modern artist deviates from the accepted norm as a consequence of his unique thought process and original spirit. It is a deviation which causes the chasm between the existing cultural tradition and the artist's own creation. The second characteristic regards formal aspects which are affected by the respective content of either modern or classic art. Thus, for example, Burckhardt considers Michelangelo to be the first modern painter, in light of his search for new formal alternatives to depict death.[5] Burckhardt observes in the artist's original form a manifestation of individual thinking, different from its contemporary governing attitudes and inclinations, and thus labels it modernist.

Likewise, Herbert Read develops an appreciation of the modern based on quality and action, rather than the chronological principle. He draws a distinction between two prevailing art principles: the "classic," which reflects tradition and is accepted as such by society, and the "romantic," which conveys the artist's subjective expression and is independent of any previous norm.[6] Read further clarifies the dialectics of these two principles, asserting that both are two aspects of one personality, the classical aspect representing the exterior of the person, while the romantic aspect portrays the internal: the internal represents the creative artist, while the external denotes society. Read explains that this does not connote that the artist is de-tached from external reality, but that he relates to it in an entirely subjective manner that is independent of preset norms. Moreover, according to Read, in a case where the artist accepts society's way of thinking, and thereby becomes the external shell, that person is in fact no longer an artist.[7]

Given these views, it follows that the definition of modernism— as asserted in this book—does not depend on either external circum-stances or chronological data. Instead, the term is defined in the context of the artist's creativity. The modern, therefore, does not rep-resent or characterize a given period, and, it can occur at any given time.

The modern subjective style of thinking and feeling in Cara-vaggio expresses itself through four aspects, which will be discussed comprehensively in the following chapters: realism; reflection of the self in the work of art; formal equivalents; and rejection of religious dogma. I shall now offer a brief preliminary presentation of each as-pect, which is developed fully in the opening to each chapter. There the relevant theoretical and philosophical facets of each aspect are dealt with mainly by analyzing and synthesizing views of major scholars dealing with these very issues in the field of art history.

The term "realism," as used in this book, concerns a work of art in which reality is materialized through a subjective insight that stems from the artist's unique being that is committed to its introver-sion. This type of realism is filled with the artist's unique personality as a creative individual. The first chapter on realism deals with the topic by examining three paintings: *Basket of Fruit*, *The Cardsharps* and *Death of the Virgin*. The analysis employs the principle of sub-jective outlook, and reveals a different reality in comparison to other contemporary and existing traditions.

The aspect of reflection of the self is directly related to the first one. Here, the objective reality is endowed with added significance directly attributable to the spiritual, ideal, and psychological characteristics of the artist's personality. The second chapter examines this through the following paintings: *Young Sick Bacchus, Medusa* and *David with the Head of Goliath*. The objective here is to show how Caravaggio's personality is projected in the figures forming the subject of these works of art.

The third aspect, which I shall call formal equivalents, is also linked to the first two. However, while realism and reflection of the self deal with content, formal equivalents is preoccupied with the formal and attempts to clarify how the subjective view of an objective reality achieves formal expression. In other words, how the formal aspect, based on a pure formalistic language, reflects the uniqueness of the artist as a person as well as his understanding and how he captures reality. The third chapter is based on Caravaggio's *Judith Beheading Holofernes, Calling of St. Matthew* and *Conversion of St. Paul*. These paintings demonstrate how the artist's feelings and state of mind are innately expressed through formal artistic language.

Likewise, the fourth aspect, rejection of religious dogma, is directly related to the uniqueness of the artist's inner being. Religion is inevitably based on obligatory rules to be followed by the whole community of believers. Consequently, religion inherently rejects all individual interpretation, thus overcoming its fear of heresy. The modern artist, as that term is employed in this book, responds exclusively to idiosyncratic feelings and thoughts, resulting in unique personal interpretations. Therefore, the artist necessarily deviates from accepted dogma. The fourth chapter is divided into two subchapters: the first deals with the image of the saint and the works chosen are: *St. Matthew and the Angel, Crucifixion of St. Peter* and *Martyrdom of St. Matthew*; the second sub-chapter focuses on the image of Mary, as depicted in the paintings *Rest on the Flight into Egypt, Madonna of Loreto* (*Madonna of the Pilgrims*) and *Adoration of the Shepherds*. The final chapter provides a philosophical approach to the four main chapters as conclusion.

Three alternatives were considered during the research process. The first involved the presentation of Caravaggio's paintings chronologically; the second was based on a presentation of Caravaggio's painting according to their respective subjects (mythology, the New Testament, the Old Testament, genre, etc.); the third alternative concerned the method of demonstrating and concretizing the ideas stemming from the four aspects of modernism as previously discussed, with no link to dates or subjects.

The first two alternative approaches were obviously rejected after several futile attempts. Consequently, I adopted the third alternative—notwithstanding the difficulties involved—as I realized that the above four modernist aspects appear in Caravaggio's works, in a more or less emphasized manner. The choice of certain works to demonstrate these criteria may appear arbitrary at times. However, the specific works of art chosen for this purpose serve a convenient frame within which to achieve the purposes of this book.

In support of the interpretation presented above, I shall employ data obtained from Caravaggio's times. I will also use the conclusions stemming from the formal analysis of works of art, which is based on the previously described criteria defining modernism. Thus, my objective is to lend credence to the thesis embedded in the title: *Caravaggio as a Modernist* and ponder once more: *What is Modernism?*

REALISM

In the introduction I have attempted to clarify that the concept of "realism," as envisioned here, differs from its conventional definition. It does not stand for objective viewing, but includes subjective factors. Realism, as such, is subject to what the individual artist sees and understands as "real." However, there is an additional factor, which equally contributes to the concept realism: the viewer who looks at the work of art which the artist comprehends as being realistic. In effect, does the viewer, a different subject, see the work through the artist's eyes? Alternatively, does the viewer deform what is seen due to that person's own way of thinking?

Roman Jacobson deals with this complex issue in his essay, "On Realism in Art." Jacobson's underlining premise is that realism is an artistic style aiming to present reality most truthfully possible and with the highest reasonableness: we denominate realistic works of art which present reality with reasonable truthfulness.[1] If one accepts this definition as valid, the question arises whether this "reasonable truthfulness" to reality refers to the artist's intentions or to the viewer's, who grasps this reality as acceptable. In the discussion on the artist's way of presenting reality, an additional question is necessarily posed: does the artist believe that the work is reasonably truthful to reality if it deviates from contemporaneous conventional and artistic norms of society or does the artist adopt a more conservative attitude regarding art and reality?

The same question is obviously relevant in reference to the viewer: is the viewer revolutionary in comparison to contemporaneous conventions of society or conservative in thought and practice regarding approaches to social conventions? Jacobson comprehends the work of art as realist according to its being reasonably truthful to reality as grasped by both artist and viewer. Thus, he definitely abolishes the meant-to-be "objective" criteria in reference to the meaning of realism in art.

Thomas Munro differentiates between realism and naturalism in art. Accordingly, naturalism is the style which represents nature, including man and his creations, by emphasizing the externally seen, as well as the behavior outwardly exposed. The theory which supports naturalism claims that truth is reflected through facts. Therefore, art obligatorily has to deal with these facts, which are of the highest value, more significant than beauty or nobility. Likewise, realism deals with facts, but while naturalism emphasizes the externally seen, realism departs from the external, only to reach deeper meanings. The term "naturalism" or "realism" depends on the person who is concerned, as well as that person's comprehending of the goals and value of art.[2] Much like Jacobson, then, Munro does not grant a single meaning to the term realism, relying on definite objective factors, but relates the term to the subject who experiences reality and interprets it.

In her book on realism, Linda Nochlin analyzes the complexity of the term. Throughout her book on nineteenth-century Realism she accentuates the idea of the subjective aspect in it.[3] The first question posed by Nochlin is philosophical: is reality truthful and concrete in its own value or is it not but an illusion in the eyes of the beholder? Are we dealing with eternal essences, or with concrete phenomena? When dealing with phenomena received through visual experience—is this experience permanent and objective in itself, or is it comprehended as being altered by time and space?

The second question is directly linked to the world of art: since the artistic creation constitutes a link between the artist's experience and the viewer's, and since the viewer is not subject to the particular circumstances under which the artist created, that viewer might interpret the work of art in a different way. Nochlin concludes that there is no one absolute reality and no one unique way to perceive it.[4] Nochlin, as the previous mentioned scholars, concludes that there is no one decisive and objective reality, as reality is relative to both creator and viewer.

Thus, nineteenth-century Realism is not to be solely perceived according to the innocent eye but according to the temperament of the viewer, independently of the tradition of the past. Such eyes choose to avoid prefixed pictorial schemes and thus keep their freshness and spontaneity.[5] Nochlin proceeds to clarify that the way of perception based on the temperament of the perceiving subject has consequences reflected in several domains. The first, an approach to history free of metaphysical and ethical interpretations based on concrete facts; the second, preference of the actual based on the present, rather than interpretations deriving from the past; and, thirdly, legitimacy to deal with daily and routine issues linked to the contemporary. Discussing heroism along the periods, Nochlin writes that the nineteenth-century hero in art, contrarily to his predecessors, has to persuade through his truthfulness and genuineness.[6] Thus, his value and importance are linked to his times and not necessarily to external factors, as beauty or glory. The realist nineteenth-century hero may come from low or high social strata; in both cases, he is equally treated.

At the outset of the introduction, I have discussed modernism and its ambivalence, and proposed an alternative interpretation based on values and not on chronological survey, values here meaning the singularity of thought characteristic to modernism. According to Nochlin, nineteenth-century Realism differs from convention,[7] due to its subjectivity and therefore corresponds to the definition of modernism as suggested in this book.[8]

Stéphane Mallarmé understands modernism as the ability to confide in fresh eyes untainted by the past; the conventional way should be put aside and "the naturalist way" should be adapted.[9] The past is to serve solely as inspiration while primordial significance is to be granted to the existent. Therefore, the artist must develop a personal point of view, in order to attain truth, simplicity, and a child-like fascination. Art has to draw its inspiration from the present and reflect it as politics or industry, becoming an integral a part of life. Originality, concludes Mallarmé, can be born only by reviving perceptions based on personal senses.

Similarly to Nochlin and Mallarmé, Meyer Shapiro in his book, *Modern Art: Nineteenth and Twentieth Centuries*, amply discusses Courbet's choice of the anti-hero in comparison to tradition. From now on, the primitive and naïve elements will be validated; true creativity may derive from folklore, concludes Shapiro.[10] Regarding primitive elements, Nochlin explains that there is a significant difference between romanticism and realism in the nineteenth century.[11] Romanticism considered these primitivist elements not as a goal per se, but as means of presenting other contents, even transcendental ones. Realism treated the same elements as being directly linked to a truthful knowledge of the contemporary and thus helped to free art from its previous metaphysical and normative chains, as expressed in the subject of death. Transcendental beliefs, emotions, and even eschatological beliefs are replaced by the existent as it is. Realism shows death with no ennoblement, beautification, or holiness.

The legitimacy to draw inspiration from daily reality enables a new perception, new heroes pertaining to daily life, primitive and folklore elements—all part of routine existence. Daily materials and direct perception of the real stimulate honesty, which, according to Nochlin, is the true aim of art.[12]

In this chapter, I discuss how the specific realism is impregnated by the artist's personality, and is linked to the modern due to subjective characteristics. Subjective realism deviates from convention and finds an original way to present traditional subjects by relying on the actually seen and by emphasizing realistic aspects. I also show how the style based on the actual and concrete as an integral part of the work of art is relevant when drawing divine or saintly figures, treated by Caravaggio as if they were simple mortals, belonging to daily experience. Caravaggio treats daily subjects with no spiritual contents and vice versa—paints holy subjects as if they were secular, while avoiding attributes which by convention indicate the divine, holy or transcendental, and instead, adheres to transitory material and to concreteness. Lastly, I stress that by ignoring traditional traits, painting martyrdom or divine figures with realism and crudity, Caravaggio does not leave any possibility for salvation.

In the painting *Basket of Fruit* (fig. 1) the bowl is placed over an emphasized bottom line, which serves both as the bowl's support and the contour line of the painting. The bowl is placed in the center of the composition, but some of the fruits tend to surpass the frame. The background is painted in a uniform neutral bright color. The fruits and their leaves are painted with naturalism, in contrast to the structural and abstract perception of the composition. This perception has undergone a process of diminution and selection of essential motifs granting both a sense of flatness and illusion of depth.[13] Therefore, a polarity is created between a still-life tending to the figurative, and an abstract composition and background.

The stress on the figurative aspect caused the Marchese Vincenzo Giustiniani (1564–1637), a contemporary of Caravaggio's, to write that Caravaggio says he invests the same effort in making a good painting of fruits as in making figures.[14] This statement, to which I shall return shortly, is a key to a different understanding of Caravaggio's perception. With reference to the subject, it is clear that he follows the earlier tradition in usage of the plastic aspect and ico-nography.[15]

From the point of view of iconography, it is clear that Cara-vaggio uses traditional symbolism. The fruits here displayed are red and white grapes, apples, figs and grenades. These are autumn fruits, ranging from the ripeness of summer and verging on decay, by the scourges of insects and wilting. These fruits have not been chosen at random. The apple and figs symbolize the fruit of the Tree of Knowledge; the red and white grapes symbolize the sprout of blood and the water that flowed out of the body of Christ; and the grenade is but a symbol of the resurrection of Jesus.[16]

Nevertheless, whenever fruits or flowers appear as being ravaged by time, the iconography changes completely. Flowers and fruits like these accompanied sometimes by a skull or a vessel from which water gushes forth symbolize emptiness, *vanitas*, the material world, and its possessions.[17] Caravaggio chooses fruits with a positive mean-ing but treats them following the *vanitas* tradition.[18] He does not ig-nore the traditional motifs, but uses them in a personal, original way. This usage suggests new meanings.

In his book on early Netherlandish painting, Erwin Panofsky writes about fifteenth-century realism and symbolism. His main point relates to the dialectics between the will to reflect the visual world, as it is revealed to the artist's eyes, and the religious world to be elucidated from what is revealed.[19] The difficulty in understanding the artists' intentions is resolved by acquaintance with the current traditions of his time, according to Panofsky. In his book about un-derstanding landscape, Kenneth Clark addresses the problematic in finding out the pure "naturalistic" intentions of the artist, as well as the accompanying "disguised symbolism" of Panofsky.[20] Both Panof-sky and Clark deal with the revealed and the hidden meanings, as the latter are decipherable, being related to an acknowledged symbolic tradition.

Caravaggio, however, utilizes iconography in a unique manner.

He uses the motif of fruits, symbolizing eternity and resurrection in a context of *vanitas*, denoting materialism. The "decoding" of his work cannot be based on symbolism relating to the collective, so a new "code" must be developed, based on his unique imagination.[21]

In his book, *The Waning of the Middle Ages*, Johan Huizinga analyzes the concept of *vanitas* and concludes that paintings relating to this theme indicate non-religiosity, man's impotence to detach from material riches and thus man's incapacity to have faith:

> A thought, which so strongly attaches to the earthly side of death can hardly be called truly pious. It would rather seem a kind of spasmodic reaction against an excessive sensuality. In exhibiting the horrors awaiting all human beauty, already lurking below the surface of corporeal charms, these preachers of contempt for the world express, indeed, a very materialistic sentiment, namely, that all beauty and all happiness are worthless *because* they are bound to end soon. Renunciation founded on disgust does not spring from Christian wisdom.[22]

By uniting symbols of resurrection and death, Caravaggio, in fact, rebels against religious dogma, while using traditional collective formal language.[23] The deviation from tradition is enhanced by Caravaggio's statement quoted by Vincenzo Giustiniani which I mentioned earlier. By stating that Caravaggio invests the same effort in making a good painting of fruits as in making (holy) figures, art's commitment to religion is questioned, and the hierarchy between religious and profane motifs is cancelled: the future artist will paint whatever his eye pleases.[24] Hibbard points to yet another important aspect of Caravaggio—deviating from collective tradition and turning inwardly make him a sort of poetic innovator.[25] André Chastel writes that Caravaggio initiates a new era. From now on, the painterly discipline will extend to each and every object the eye wishes to see as a motif for painting.[26]

Following Nochlin,[27] I would venture even further and suggest that the freedom in the expression of the self and in choosing the content for the work of art both foresee abstraction.[28] Michael Kitson, too, links Caravaggio to modernism, as the first artist to disregard the classical conventions of beauty, whereas the good is fair and vice versa.[29] Discussing Caravaggio's religious themes in chapter 4, I will stress this feature in his work even further.

The ideas that have been put forward here link Caravaggio to modernism in his different personal use of traditional iconography, as he brings to the fore the importance of idiosyncratic creativity and imagination. In addition, free of any moralizing prejudices, he opens himself and his art to new content, and redefines beauty and ugliness as he sees fit. These matters will be analyzed further in discussing the paintings *The Cardsharps* and *Death of the Virgin*.

The Cardsharps (fig. 5) depicts two crooks cheating an innocent boy. The spectator takes part in the event due to the composition of the painting. The boy sits with his face turned to the viewer, behind him an older youth is peeping into his cards and signaling the numbers of cards to his companion. The latter pulls out a card stuck in his belt, visible only to the viewer.

Cheating and deceiving were very widespread in Europe, and it seems that Caravaggio experienced them in his youth.[30] However, northern satirical works of art were of a different character: the figures were designed theatrically and morally conveyed non-sympathy. In contrast to the Flemish tradition, Caravaggio's figures are not described grotesquely and the act of cheating takes place in a most naturalistic way. The victim (if one can indeed deduce from the painting that he is just that) is a handsome boy; so are two swindlers. The boy is clothed modestly and on his hat is a humble, almost invisible feather; the swindlers have colorful clothes but their hats sport ostentatious feathers. Parting with tradition, then, is evident in the similar treatment of the figures. It is even possible to notice more sympathy towards the swindlers. The theme is presented in a very natural, non-theatrical manner, with no moralizing undertones, as can be found in similar paintings in Flemish art.

Hibbard stresses Caravaggio's devotion to nature, citing Giovanni Pietro Bellori (1615–1696)[31] from his book *The Lives of Modern Painters, Sculptors and Architects*: "[W]hen he [Caravaggio] was shown the most famous statues of Phidias and Glykon in order that he might use them as models, his only answer was to point toward a crowd of people, saying that nature had given an abundance of matters."[32] Bellori also claims that Caravaggio gets closer to the truth at a time when the truth had been set aside, on account of the search for an ideal of artificial beauty. By removing the beauty of color and establishing the power of hues, Caravaggio achieves the reinstitution of flesh and blood. In his opinion, the reaction to the adorned, artificial mannerism is healthy and positive, canceling an arrogant, empty form of art.[33]

Bellori's words are most meaningful and stress Caravaggio's distinctness and his unique, new perception, deviating from the existing tradition. All these may be in opposition to Bellori's perception, according to which there should be no disregarding of the code of beauty, as part of tradition, but, still, he feels one should not use artifice or paintings lacking content. Bellori understands that Caravaggio is an innovator, but is unable to truly comprehend the very meaningful consequences of Caravaggio's new way—an art devoid of a behavioral code setting defined barriers between virtue and vice. The work of art, then, deviates from traditional treatment of morals and formalistic rendering of content. That is why Hibbard claims that swindling is indeed presented in the past, but is never given such importance as in Caravaggio's work.[34]

Like *The Cardsharps*, *Death of the Virgin* (fig. 6) reflects the borrowing of traditional motifs in order to convey a different message. Mary lies on her deathbed, her swollen, lifeless body gracelessly cast, her right hand placed weakly on her stomach, while the left one is hanging at her side. Her dress is slightly raised and her coarse feet revealed. The head is uncovered and the hair dispersed. It looks as if the Madonna died like any other mortal, and with no supernatural aura. A life full of suffering and pain seems to have come to an end. The apostles stand on her right, some look at her, their heads and backs bent by sorrow, some weep, their eyes hidden from the unpleasant view. There are those withdrawn, and those who quietly talk.

Mary Magdalene sits on a low bench at the left side of the Madonna, bent over her knees, her face hidden, completely immersed in deep mourning. No superfluous objects are depicted, except the deathbed, a chair, a water basin and a curtain whose design echoes the curve created by the rhythm of the apostles' heads, falling from left to right until it reaches the horizontal line of Mary, lying. The figure of the Magdalene is an opposite curve to that of the curtain. Figures and composition seem to enhance the inevitable descent towards death. The few details help to stress the descending line, rendering a feeling of oppression and doom.

Among many varying traditions and beliefs over the centuries associated with Mary and the event of her death, I shall mentioned only a few that are relevant, as they are manifested in many works of art depicting her death and are treated differently by Caravaggio. According to the Apocrypha, an angel appeared to Mary when she was sixty-years-old, holding a palm frond picked in Paradise.[35] The angel told her that the palm was to be borne before her bier three days after her death. Thereafter she would ascend to Heaven, and be crowned as Queen of Heaven. Upon the angel's return to Heaven, the palm shined like the morning star, signaling future events. The apostles, who were scattered around the world to promulgate Jesus' teachings, felt a strong, mysterious impulse and found themselves assembled in Mary's room. On the third hour of the night, Jesus appeared with angels, virgins, confessors, and a host of saints. While the heavenly chorus was heard, the Son told his Mother to join Him in Heaven, for she was chosen to reign there as queen. It is also of importance to mention that in the fourteenth and fifteenth centuries, the humanity of Mary as the suffering mother was emphasized and presented as *Mater Dolorosa*, whose death cannot be compared to any mortal's.

In his book, Hibbard presents an illustration from a book by Nadal from 1593, in which the Madonna is seen dying in her bed, surrounded by the apostles and above her, Jesus and his entourage welcome her soul (fig. 7).[36] In this illustration, her body is wrapped, the arms straightened, the covered head raised by a pillow. Mary is here shown with the sanctity befitting her traditional iconographic portrayal and according to wide-spread beliefs and traditions as mentioned above. Additional examples from the sixteenth century of a similar pattern are *The Death of the Virgin* by Joos van Cleve (fig. 9) and *The Death of the Virgin* by Peter Breugel (fig. 10). Although Breugel does not concretize the heavenly retinue, Mary's sanctity is expressed by the aura of light surrounding her prostrated image and stressed by the dark background involving the many mourners. A last example is a drawing by Dürer (fig. 11) from the beginning of the sixteenth century, featuring Mary lying covered on her bed, her head raised on a pillow, holding the candle of faith.[37]

Now in Caravaggio's *Death of the Virgin* there is no hint to the sacredness and singularity of the event. Giulio Mancini (1558–1630)[38] comments in *c.* 1617–21 that Caravaggio's painting was not accepted by the Carmelites from the Santa Maria della Scala church in Rome because the Virgin's image was based on the figure of a prostitute known to the artist.[39] Giovanni Baglione (1566–1643)[40] writes that the work had been rejected by the Carmelites because the Madonna's image is presented without sanctity or glory, her body swollen, and the feet are bare.[41] Eventually, the work was bought by the Duke of Mantua and exposed in his gallery.[42]

All this point to the conclusion that Caravaggio's *Death of the Virgin*—as his two other works previously dealt with—relies upon tradition and accepted iconography only as a starting point. Nevertheless, accepted attributes are absent; traditional depiction of the scene is rejected; the number of figures diminishes; and the aura of sanctity or uniqueness of the event is played down. Although Caravaggio retains and conveys feelings associated with the scene in a very realistic way, this realism is based only on what is seen, while giving up any transcendental or moralizing dimensions. This is, of course, all the more reason for churchmen and art critics alike to vex their indignation over Caravaggio's work.

REFLECTION OF THE SELF

In the last chapter I have discussed the way Caravaggio does not neglect traditional iconography altogether in respect of his choice of subject-matter, but at the same time, breaks away with it, choosing his own subjective and original world-view to be expressed in his work, without opting for moralizing or specific dogmatic religious connotations.

This chapter extends the idea of the previous by dealing with the synthesis between the external reality and the artist's subjective reality, and how it is visually expressed in the work of Caravaggio. As envisaged in this book, the concept of realism is that in which reality is seen only through the singular and untainted eyes of the artist, a mode of perception which is not disconnected from personality and personal experiences. This fact obligatorily infiltrates the subjective factor into the work of art. Thus, the work of art includes both the object, as part of reality, and the subject, the internal world of the creator.

In his essay on "L'art philosophique," Baudelaire considers the modern work of art to be a sort of suggestive enchantment, due to the intertwining of subject and object.[1] In his essay on the portrait, written for the Salon of 1859, Baudelaire further exemplifies the link between subject and object, reality and creator. Accordingly, the more concrete reality is, the more subjective function is involved,

because imagination has to be more active.[2] In other words, whenever reality seems as if it were easy to reconstitute, because of its concreteness, the artist has to increase his imaginary capacity.

The idea of intertwining the subjective factor and the objective
description of reality, and the link of the same intertwining with
modernism, is discussed by Robert Rosenblum in his book, *Cubism
and Twentieth-Century Art*. Rosenblum claims that in the twentieth
century, unlike the Renaissance period, there is no illusion of one
unique reality. There is a refusal to supply one meaning to the existent. In fact, the twentieth century and the Middle Ages have one
thing in common: their pictorial language refers to reality by means
of a concept.[3]

Rosemblum differs between Renaissance collective symbolism, a
result of general consent, and the subjective symbolism dependent
on the will of the creator. Furthermore, the author discusses another
significant issue. In his opinion, Modern art, which relies on subjective symbolism, resembles medieval art, for in both a conceptual
pictorial image indicating a particular reality is evident. However, the
difference consists in the fact that while the medieval concept describes reality basing itself on collective symbolism, the modern
concept can be comprehended only by being largely acquainted with
the symbolical corpus of a given artist.

Rosenblum, as Nochlin, links modernism to a system of values
deduced from the subjective state of mind. This is why he, too, sees
in Romanticism a prelude to Modern art. In his book, *Modern
Painting and the Northern Romantic Tradition*, Rosenblum discusses
the theme of nature as it is presented in the Romantic work of art.
There, nature is a combination of the existent and the artist's point of
view.[4] Naturalism wishes to capture the real and the objective, while
the subjective—as a personal point of view—brings forth the abstract
thought finding its expression in the work of art.

Rosemblum emphasizes the link between Romanticism and
modernism due to the synthesis which unites the objective and the

subjective in the work of art.[5] This synthesis enables the co-existence of two poles as the abstract and the empirical, the universal and the particular, the finite and the infinite, the microcosms and the macrocosms.[6] At times, the co-existence of the poles often expresses restlessness, and the awareness of the individual to the fact that one confronts a reality not entirely understood and therefore, one wishes to find its place in the mysterious creation. Alternatively, one would look for an explanation of a particular phenomenon, which will serve as a code to decipher the cosmic whole.

Likewise, Pheobe Pool mentions in her book, *Impressionism*, the contribution of Romanticism to Impressionism. This contribution is reflected in the formal domain as well as in the contents.[7] Romanticism freed painting from a strict formalism and over elaboration. Regarding the content, the artist's personality becomes the object of interest. The artist is in constant struggle against normative ideas and thoroughly examines the aspect of the new and unknown. Again, there is a connection between Pool's ideas and my book dealing with subjective realism, for it shows that modernism is linked to the value of the subjective, constituting the departing point for the artistic creation.

In his book on Romanticism, Hugh Honour brings forth similar ideas. In his opinion, the romantic artist is reluctant to accept symbols that underwent a codification process granting a unilateral meaning. The romantic artist chooses to be free and uses symbols at his will which derive from tradition or any other domain and aspect of life. The romantic work of art is, first and foremost, the expression of a personal point of view.[8] Honour, Rosemblum, and Pool see the connection between Romanticism and personal artistic freedom. The artist uses given formal symbols and loads them with personal meanings deriving from his unique personality.

In *On the Philosophy of Modern Art*, Read quotes Nahum Gabo who is also of the opinion that modern art is necessarily a synthesis including the subjective and the objective aspects.[9] According to

Gabo, if one assumes that there is an infiltration of the self in the work of art, one must also conclude that the perceived is but a reflection of the specific viewing self. Gabo does not associate himself with those who stand for philosophical theories believing that art has to reveal an eternal truth, a truth existing as a universal substance, independently of the thinking subject.[10]

Gabo also does not pertain to those who believe that by acquiring knowledge they reveal reality as it is. A stable and pure reality, for whatever man has knowledge of is but a construction of his own. This cannot exist *ex persona* and cannot be part of a transcendental reality. Reality is an assemblage of images impossible to interpret Platonically, for they do not refer to an ideal and transcendental reality, as there is nothing existing beyond them. The images simply stand for what they are. Read quotes Gabo in order to stress the importance of the self in modern philosophy. The "self" decides how to see reality and paints it according to its inner colors.[11]

I now move on to demonstrate how Caravaggio's singular personality is mirrored in his paintings through the synthesis between naturalism, revealing correspondence to the objective external reality, and the subjectivity of the creator, coloring naturalism with its own nuances. Caravaggio's feelings as a victim, for instance, influence his approach to the traditional hero. He turns the hero into an anti-hero, and the figure depicted attracts sympathy, though according to tradition it meant to carry negative connotations. The concealed meanings transmitted through the works have only an apparent affinity to traditional iconography.

Moreover, the common description of saints and the positive one of crooks inspiring empathy points to a violation of the moral norm in the artist's era. I also touch upon his sexual inclinations and the way they color his boyish figures. To summarize, I show Caravaggio's high awareness to his problematic person, mirroring his soul both as a performer of sacrifices and as a victim. I wish to stress Caravaggio's impact on his own work, very unusual in his times.

Young Sick Bacchus (fig. 12) sits with his body turned aside, the head towards the viewer. His expression and smile recall the inscrutable face of the *Mona Lisa*, but his gaze wanders, unfocused, shrouded by melancholy. The figure is placed on one side of the table, while the potential looker stands perforce on the other side. The composition is similar to that of *The Cardsharps*, as in both instances the viewer is involved. The picture frame cuts the schematically painted table and the fruits that "fall" out of the lower line. Bacchus is described as a youngster crowned by ivy leaves holding a bunch of grapes. On the table are red grapes and two peaches. Despite the muscular body displayed by the god through the classical toga, Bacchus seems ill. The color of his flesh resembles an over-ripe peach. The dark grapes stress this ripeness. The pale body is emphasized by the dark neutral background.

The vacant gaze invites certain reactions, through the parted bluish lips, fleshy and somewhat swollen, the pose conveying softness and femininity. The contrast between the dark background and the pale body, and between the peach and the grapes, induces tension. It is not surprising then, that when comparing the tenebrism prevailing in Caravaggio's works with that of his followers, Germain Bazin claims that there is a significant difference between the source and the latter. Caravaggio's darkness does not intend to swallow or fog the figures, but to stress their density.[12]

The figure stands out due to its plastic design, as well as to its contents. An unpleasant feeling is conveyed by the femininity of the boy's appearance. Kitson decisively states that Caravaggio's boys infer an erotic aspect, and are the product of a homosexual artist, working for patrons having the same inclinations.[13]

However, the painting was possibly made soon after Caravaggio's recovery from a severe illness. Roberto Longhi claims that the painting is the artist's self-portrait, made soon after his release from the hospital, where he was interned with malaria.[14] On the other hand, Mancini claims that Caravaggio fell sick after being kicked by a horse. Gash suggests that the figure relates to the elegiac poet D'arfino with whose circle Caravaggio was acquainted (D'arfino was described in Alcianti's popular poem *Emblemata*).[15]

The views of Caravaggio's contemporaries—as are those of modern scholars—vary in their interpretation of this piece. However, a common ground can be found in their noticing the god's irregular treatment by the artist. He might be sexually deviant, physically ill or portraying an elegiac poet, however, he does not confirm with Bacchus' descriptions in Greek mythology. Greek mythology presents Bacchus as the god of wine and fertility. His rituals were accompanied by wild orgies. The animal sacrificed to him was torn to pieces and its flesh eaten raw by the worshipers, symbolizing the consumption of the god's flesh. Mostly, women tended to worship Bacchus. They danced, beat drums, freed from any physical or moral restraints. According to traditional iconography, Bacchus is usually portrayed wearing a wreath of vine and ivy leaves and holding a cup of wine.

Humanists referred to Bacchus as the ideological counterpart of Apollo. The first represented for them instincts, and the latter symbolized reason. Bacchus represents the irrational in human nature, the remaining animal instincts.[16] Renaissance painters usually describe Bacchus accompanied by goats, maenads, satyrs and the old drunken Silenus or the god Pan. They generally express an abandonment of the body to a mood of inflamed passions, panic, and other mysterious influences.[17] There is no doubt that the body is the recipient of psychic beings. In his book on the nude, Kenneth Clark reviews the various poses of the naked body, and divides them into four kinds. His second category, "the ecstatic," is that where the will is defeated while the body is controlled by the irrational. In this state, there is no stability or response to physical laws. However, if the body does not lose its balance, it is due to its inherent enthusiasm.[18] The characteristics of Bacchus are formally concretized in the ecstatic nude as it is depicted in Titian's *Bacchus and Ariadne*. His figure seems to be hovering in the air in a forward swing. The traditional entourage thrusts forward, enveloped in ecstasy, driven by their instincts. The god himself is shown naked, his cloak wildly fluttering behind, the hands thrust forward, the hair unkempt, the mouth open and the eyes gazing passionately at his beloved, whose back is turned to the viewer, while she breaks out of the lower right part of the painting. Titian does not leave any doubt to the fact that the god Bacchus is depicted here, with all his power, instincts, sensuality, and wildness.

Unlike Titian's, Caravaggio's Bacchus is represented as an elegiac, lifeless figure, unaccompanied by any other figure. This utterly different depiction of the god is the reason behind doubts concerning its identity. It has a crown of ivy leaves, instead of the traditional wreath of vine and ivy leaves, and the cup of wine generally held by the god is missing. All These deviations point out the difficulty in attaching a definite identity to the figure.[19]

Young Sick Bacchus could well represent Bacchus because of its similarity to Caravaggio's other *Bacchus* (fig. 13) in clothing and androgynous features. Again, it could even be a self-portrait expressing the artist's illness, his physical and spiritual penchants.[20] The seeming simple presentation of the subject, then, becomes more complex after deeper observation. Evidently, the link between the form and its symbol is not easily decoded.[21]

Discrepancies in iconographic attributes and positive identification of the figure in the painting to one side, more important for my purposes here is that Caravaggio can be compared to modernism, for the symbol, as introduced above, is entirely dependent upon the uniqueness of the artist's spirit and way of thinking. It seems as if the artist rebels against the valid iconographic norms and follows his inspired and imaginative creativity. He, therefore, may be considered a "romantic" according to definitions of such an artist. Honour, as I showed earlier,[22] stresses that a romantic certainly moves away from any norm as part of being a spontaneously creative and enthusiastic individual. Baudelaire, too, sustains that Romanticism is a way of feeling, more than a choice of subjects, or an exact reconstruction of a precise truth. The French term *"romantisme"* describes a state of mind which may be translated as "introversion," "spirituality," "color," "a striving for infinity"—and these are expressed by all the means existing in the different art domains. Due to the subjective character of Romanticism, Baudelaire does not hesitate to link this trend with Modernism, self-assuredly stating that "[q]ui dit romantisme, dit art moderne."[23]

In two other works one can witness a way of reference to reality which expresses the artist's uniqueness of soul. *Medusa* (fig. 14) is depicted with blood running out of her slain neck and gaping mouth. The eyes are wide open and the knitted brows create creases in its young front. Terrifying snakes wound around the head, becoming part of it. The teeming snake-hair turns everywhere.

The mythological Medusa Gorgon is one of three Gorgon sisters, daughters of Phorcys. These sisters were so horrid—their eyes protruded, the mouths grew canine teeth, their tongues shot out, and instead of hair snakes grew—that anyone looking at them turned to stone and died. Assisted by Hermes and Pallas-Athena, Perseus succeeded in cutting off the Medusa's head. Nevertheless, even after death, the monster remained powerful, and its image was carved on warrior shields. Thus, the shield was used as a weapon against the enemy, and the protector of its bearer. In *Metamorphoses*, Ovid often mentions the powerful shield featuring Medusa's head. Perseus, in one of his adventures, held the shield in front of the giant Atlas. Atlas immediately became a mountain, his beard and hair forests, his shoulders hills, his head the summit, his bones turned into rocks and thereafter, heaven and the luminaries were placed upon. Some other time, Phineus begs Perseus to turn away his shield, as the Medusa's head converts everything into marble.[24] Thus the monster terrifies and spreads death everywhere.

Friedlaender states that the Medusa image depicted by Caravaggio is based on a type commonly used in the Archaic and Etruscan periods. In those times, the monster tends to express its distorted nature, in opposition to later periods, in which the Medusa's image was depicted in a more appealing way.[25] Discussing this, Michael Avi-Yonah writes in his book, *A History of Classical Art*, that the Greeks inherited their monsters from Mesopotamian cultures, but toned down the intensity of their looks, until they became refined images, as the feminine, dreamlike Sphinx of Thebes, or other winged symbols.[26]

The external look of the Medusa is linked to its iconography, for her classical role is to turn her enemy into stone. However, there are deeper philosophical aspects. In his 1593 edition of *Iconologia*, Ripa refers to the monster as a symbol of man's enemies, who actually are a part of his inner being and very essence.[27] These enemies represent the physical aspect of the senses, the senses being the natural foe of Virtue. The Medusa is bound to turn these internal enemies into stone, as though they were physical ones. Another significance is one probably reflecting the moral aspect. The Medusa's head is linked to the disillusion that hardens the heart of man and does not allow him to repent. It is to be supposed therefore that Caravaggio is aware of the diverse iconographic explanations linked to the monster, as well as of its traditional ways of representation. A more profound observation reveals an intriguing deviation from convention, though.

Contrary to the monster generally depicted by tradition, not only does Caravaggio's Medusa not terrify the viewer, but is itself terrified by the menacing snakes bustling in its head, its open mouth cries and blood trickles out. The monster is actually afraid of its own mirrored reflection.[28] The situation is now reversed—the viewers are not in danger from turning ideologically into stone, instead, they are filled with compassion towards the impotency of the image. The different approach to the traditional subject necessarily changes the meanings. Caravaggio-Medusa, generally considered a wild, unbridled person, sees himself as a victim of his own singular character, and is shattered by his inner being, as concretized through the monster. Medusa is the expression of the artist's emotional state. He may be acquainted with his troublesome personality but is helpless. Much like society around him, he is mortified by the vices within him.

A similar phenomenon takes place in *David with the Head of Goliath* (fig. 15). The tent David has just come out of is hinted by a triangle in the upper left corner of the painting. The background and the triangle are dark, stressing the whiteness of the figures. Darkness-brightness may indicate the drama taking place between killer and victim. David holds in his right hand an enormous sword and in his left the just cut-off head of Goliath by the hair. He looks at his victim's head with mercy. An elegiac atmosphere pervades the painting. Goliath's giant head is still full of life, its mouth open in a last painful cry, the blood flowing as arrows from the neck, the eyes half closed, suffering, as if to emit the last cry of pain, the creases gathered in the middle of the forehead. His expression denotes bygone strength, a strong feeling of overcome power, and a sense of the finality of death.

Caravaggio's different approach to the subject of David and Goliath can be grasped when compared to David sculpted by Donatello, Verrocchio and Michelangelo. Donatello's *David* of 1431–3 (fig. 16) is a handsome youth, with long curls covered by a splendid wide-brimmed hat, the posture is arrogant, ostentatious and graceful, his leg trampling with ease and confidence Goliath's head, thrown as a useless object. The viewer is naturally attracted by the victor's refined image, while the defeated is just an iconographic attribute.

Verrocchio's *David* of 1461 (fig. 17) is tenser and more muscular, entirely lacking any mannerism and his sword is decisively held. This David is convincing in his ability to cut the head off of his enemy. Nevertheless, the two sculptures have common aspects: David appears as a confident young man.

Michelangelo's *David* of 1501–4 (fig. 18) is not depicted as a youth. Like Donatello's *David*, he stands naked but does not wear high boots or a decorated hat. Neither does his hair fall gracefully over the shoulders. His stance is frontal, the head turning to the left. Contrary to the other sculptures, Michelangelo does not leave any hint of Goliath's head. His David is alert, the right arm stretched along the body, the big sized hand turns inward, the left arm bends forward holding a sling, the right leg deviates from the central axis. The facial traits are sharp with eyes alert as an eagle on his prey.

A confident, victorious David, as perceived by the three artists, is in accordance to the scriptures that carry a meaningful, clear message: God, and not human physical strength, shall determine who is to live and who is to lose. Michelangelo's *David* expresses his confidence in God in every single limb. In her book on Michelangelo, Linda Murray discusses further ideas. The Florentines considered *David* as symbol of the perfect citizen—courageous, strong, and faithful.[29] Murray compares Michelangelo's David to Hercules, who succeeded to overcome all obstacles due to his physical and spiritual abilities. She goes on to discuss his unique appearance as meaningful. This David is extrospective and not introspective. This is in line with medieval conceptions that saw the extrospective as passive and the introspective as active. David needs no earthly sword since he puts his trust in the Lord.[30]

Like in previous instances, Caravaggio follows the traditional iconography, laden with meanings, providing his own interpretation. Based on Bellori and Manilli, Friedlaender states that the figure of Goliath is a portrait of the elder Caravaggio, while David's portrays the image of the younger artist.[31] The artist deals with his subject-matter similarly to that of *Medusa* and *Judith Beheading Holofernes* (fig. 19).[32] The boundaries between murderer and murdered are blurred. David the victorious, much like Medusa, is victim of his own deeds. If in *Medusa*, representing the artist's self-portrait, Caravaggio is compelled to use a mirror, in *David with the Head of Goliath* he

uses the mirror as an idea. Caravaggio seems to realize the impossi-
bility to be free of existential entanglements: the young Caravaggio
looks at the adult Caravaggio becoming quarrelsome, arrogant, and
belligerent, disdaining the laws of society, an escaped murderer con-
stantly fleeing trial.[33]

In the chapter on Caravaggio's realism I have stressed the artist's
reliance on tradition but at the same time giving his work meaning
that moves away from it, concentrating instead on the empirically
existent. This chapter draws a similar conclusion: the figures of
Bacchus, Medusa, Goliath, and David are treated according to the
artist's own spirit, mental capacities and moods. In Caravaggio,
Bacchus, the lubricious god of fertility, turns into an androgynous
character, on the verge of decay and degeneracy; Medusa, the mur-
derous monster—into an effeminate youth, appalled by the snakes
writhing on her head; the formidable Goliath—into an elderly man
pitted even by his young slayer; while David, the killer as it were, and
not victoriously so, turns into a victim, unwillingly taking a life,
mournfully poring over the outcome of the action of his own hand.

FORMAL EQUIVALENTS

In the two previous chapters I have tried to demonstrate how Caravaggio's uniquely creative personality manifested itself in his work as well as in his own subjective grasp of reality. These chapters mainly dealt with content as working through typical and collective iconography while deviating from that very tradition in order to advance a subjective point of view. This subjective note aided me in placing Caravaggio as fit to be called a modernist.

The present chapter runs along the same line of thought, while concentrating on the formal aspects of the works, rather than their content. It seeks to show how the formal is an autonomously form of expression of content. It is not just means in the service of a more important content, but, on the contrary, is equal to it, while employing a pure artistic language of painting. Hence, these "formal equivalents," as I term them, also serve to tie Caravaggio to modernism, owing to the subjective imprinting in the artistic endeavor itself.

To define this term, I rely on Maurice Denis' theory on art. Denis considers the formal means used by the artist as most meaningful. Contrary to Émile Zola, who defines art as "nature seen through the temperament," Denis is of the opinion that the work of art is founded on pure artistic means: line, color, surface, composition, etc., which form the plastic equivalents of the objects perceived, as well as the artist's inner feelings and states of mind.[1]

In *A Concise History of Modern Sculpture* Read exposes a possible meaning to modernism by analyzing formal aspects and discusses the ability to create forms in relation to the spirit of their times. Such a capacity is modernism.[2] Similarly, in *The Tradition of the New*, Harold Rosenberg proposes that to be a modern is not a condition, but an effort, an effort to reject forms which time had invalidated, and are no more suitable to contain the ideas of their times or, alternatively, an effort to modify the existent forms, according to the emerging new needs.[3]

Both Read and Rosenberg consider the changing of the plastic form of expression a must which necessarily accompanies a shift in ways of thought or in a general state of mind. The individual perception deviates from the conventional and materializes in a new plastic language which, likewise, differs from the conventional formal language.

In his *Philosophy of Modern Art* Read studies the issue of plastic equivalents by comparing Picasso to Juan Gris. In the phase of Analytic Cubism, Picasso's starting point is the surrounding reality. However, he aims to find a structural and schematic order in his objects. Nevertheless, when the vital and the organic characteristics of the objects are endangered by the mentioned structural and schematic treatment, Picasso retreats, abandons this way, and does not accomplish full abstraction. It seems that at a certain critical phase, when the artist feels that the formal means cease to function as equivalents to his realistic perception, he withdraws on the edge of carrying out abstraction.[4]

In contrast to Picasso, Read indicates, Gris chooses a divergent starting point, anchored in abstraction. For him, the work of art is indebted to its abstract factors, as form and color. These components are what he calls its "architecture." The work of art begins its life with a formal arrangement of the pictorial surface. Only in a more advanced stage Gris introduces the representational elements. The abstract constituents of the work are called "the architecture" and represent a mathematical perception on the part of the artist. The mathematical perception, relying on abstract factors, serves to accentuate the figurative elements drawn from the surrounding reality. The figurative comes into effect by means of the previous formal arrangement, as well as by the structuring of the composition.[5]

The sculptor Barbara Hepworth has a similar way of thinking. There is for her no difference, neither in intention nor in state of mind, when she paints and sculpts in a realistic manner or in the abstract. Both manners offer the same happiness, sorrow, or joy, dwelling in the line, form, and color. In both manners she experiences a search for something.[6] Intermingling effortlessly, the two artistic expressions grant mutual strength by enabling absolute freedom, so as to complete the circle. The realistic manner responds to the existent need of loving life, humanity, and the earth, while the abstract one sharpens the personality and the senses, so the perception of life becomes more integral and imbued by an internal intention. Hepworth makes a simultaneous usage of formal means linked either to reality or to abstraction.

Rosenblum states that Cubism assumes that the work of art does not function as a reference to a transcendental reality but represents an autonomous reality—one which exemplifies the process through which nature becomes art.[7] In the new substantiality created by Cubism there is no absolute finality. An object whose form is solid and opaque becomes in art an object depicted as being transparent and weightless. Similarly, a right and stable line in nature might dissolve in the artistic language and become a quivering texture. Thus, the identity of the objects may succumb to various meanings having no definite, unequivocal, and unique significance. In times concerned with definite truths and essences, Cubism created an artistic language with numerous meanings. The viewer looking at a cubist work of art realizes that one cannot relate to forms, textures, space, or objects in a non-complex way.

From the above, it can be concluded that the formal equivalents are a necessity for the modern artist. It is the artist who eventually chooses the forms, which most suit an inner reality. No longer are artists satisfied with a mere representation of the existent by emulation and they find an alternative way and create a new synthesis by means of the plastic equivalents. In such a synthesis, the substance of the objective and figurative reality is connected to the subjective and abstract reality, so as to create an autonomous pictorial reality.

I now turn to address formal equivalents in Caravaggio's works and how his formal language is not in accordance with the normative and conventional language of his contemporaries. Thus, he exposes his particular state of mind and way of thinking characterizing a unique human being, and an extraordinary artist. I also concentrate on how his art contains realistic and figurative aspects deriving from surrounding reality, as well as pure formal aspects, like *chiaroscuro* contrasts, artificial approach to light, and abstraction of space and time. The plastic aspects will be regarded as formal subjective equivalents, through which Caravaggio expresses his turbulence, anxiety, desires, belief, and non-belief.

In her book, *Caravage, ou L'Expérience de la matière*, Françoise Bardon deals with the subject of formal equivalents, without really defining them as such: "The search for formal, abstract schemes is necessary to Caravaggio, because he refuses to follow the literary a-prior for his paintings. Caravaggio must go through abstraction, to create a renewed acquaintance with reality, in order to invent an iconography in which the meaning is inseparable from form."[8] Bardon clarifies her words, and states that Caravaggio does paint reality, but his great value lies in his understanding that this reality passes, first of all, through the filter of abstraction—namely, through the processing of rational forms, which convey the visual perception. Therefore, she believes that with Caravaggio one must not separate between reality and its formal translation. This later on leads her to state that this artist's work is the most abstract of his times, and simultaneously, the most realistic: Caravaggio succeeds in showing the reality of his times because he objectifies reality. Caravaggio's realism is more a realism of knowledge than of direct observation. In other words, Bardon differentiates between realism of observation based only on the eye and realism that translates the seen as a rational formal whole, relying on the a-priori abstract perception. Bardon names the other type of realism "realism of knowledge," in contrast to "realism of immediate perception."[9] Realism, in the sense of knowledge, must, therefore, be abstract, as it builds its creation according to the rational composition and turns it into an independent object.[10]

Three figures appear in *Judith Beheading Holofernes* (fig. 19). Holofernes is lying in bed, creating a horizontal line that echoes the width of the painting. Judith and her servant stand one behind the other, creating vertical lines, in accord with the height of the rectangle. From the point of view of space allotment, Holofernes fills half of the painting, while the two women are placed in the other half. The element linking between the horizontal, passive block—Holofernes—and the vertical, active block—the women—are Judith's hands holding the sword and beheading the victim. The arms serve as a kind of lever. The hands of the man, surprised in his sleep, are tense and not limp, as they would naturally be expected. The right hand is holding the bed and is pressed into the sheet, out of sheer pain, while the other hand contracts its fingers. The mouth is open in an outcry as the wretched Medusa or Goliath, the eyes are open and fogged reflecting fear and suffering.

Judith is the active one, while the servant, her collaborator, holds the piece of cloth destined to wrap the slain head. Both of them are in absolute contrast to the horizontal figure. The contrast focuses not only in the polarity between vertical and horizontal lines, but also in the differences in the figures' depiction. The murderers' lips are sealed in opposition to the victim's outcry. This is a silence of resoluteness, of determination to perform the killing, come what may. This is particularly true in the case of the old servant, with her crooked nose, fallen mouth, exaggeratedly big ears and her neck resembling a sharp knife. These show an almost beastly toughness and determination, contrasting with her withering skin and thinning hair, covered by a kerchief fastened around the head, her bent body and her bony and angular hands. Judith, in comparison, features a totally different image. The younger woman's stature has not yet contracted by the hardships of life, her skin is fresh, her features are delicate and her dress enhances her femininity. Her curls, the pearl earrings, the sleeved shirt complimenting her figure and the movement of the skirt created by the thrust of the beheading are in dramatic contrast to the scene of the naked, bleeding impotent victim surprised in his sleep. The terrible deed performed in the depth of night is conspicuous not only because of the darkness characterizing the background but also because of the suddenly shifted canopy curtain, the invaded privacy, and the flow of life that was brutally cut off.

Caravaggio leaves the viewer in suspense, because the act of killing has not been completed. The blood flows as knives over the white sheet. The action will be completed only when the lever of the hands—linking between the vertical and the horizontal—returns to its original state. Judith's expression is sealed and puzzling, the tension and concentration in the act are reflected in the creases appearing in the forehead, in the bridge of the nose and in the eyes, almost sinking in their cavities. It seems as if the murderess is acting out of an external compulsion, activated by mechanic body movements, while her soul might reveal compassion. As David in *David with the Head of Goliath*, she is propelled by an inner impulse, but at the same time, is aware of the pernicious consequences of her act.[11] Caravaggio succeeds in conveying this dramatic tension to the viewer by means of a thrifty composition, based on the confrontation between one horizontal and two vertical lines, between one passive and two active elements. The lack of hope and the arisen tension derive from the choice of a killing location seemingly protected by a curtain. The viewers become accomplices and sole witnesses to the event, and naturally, will remain silent. As in *The Cardsharps*, here, too, the scene might continue beyond the margins of the painting, and the viewer gains a close view encouraging involvement, accrued by the intentional flashes of light.

The illumination is focused on the part of the naked man's body and lights up part of his face. Nevertheless, most of the figure is obscured, and may refer to the darkness of death. In comparison to the victim, the entire body of the murderess is shining. The servant, her silent accomplice, appears from Judith's left, as if thrust by the darkness.

According to the Apocrypha, Judith was a Jewish widow who saved her country when it was attacked by the Assyrian kingdom. During the Renaissance, Judith became a Catholic symbol of Fortitude—namely, spiritual fortitude. Part of Judith's prayer is included in the Catholic prayer book, where she is recalled in the context of Mary's Immaculate Conception; Judith is the savior of her people as Mary is a lifeline to her believers.[12]

Thus, Donatello's portrayal of Judith, for instance, is of a symbol of the triumph of virtue over vice (fig. 20). In contrast to this traditional perception, Caravaggio's Judith is not a symbol of spiritual fortitude. She and her servant act involuntarily, drawn by their physical, instinctive facet, and Holofernes does not represent vice. Like Caravaggio's Goliath, he is deprived of his potency, inducing to commiseration and sympathy on part of the viewer. Bardon expresses a significant idea on this subject, according to which the notion of the victim symbolizing evil and being defeated by the hero is long bygone. From now on, the difference between the virtuous and the sinner will remain unclear.[13] This blurring of limits between virtue and vice as moral parameters is reflected in the confrontation of extremes formalistically expressed: verticals versus horizontals, light against darkness, and distortion as opposing calm.

The subject of formal aspects as equivalents to content has also been discussed by Chastel. He states that a distinction should be made between the earlier works of Caravaggio and the later ones painted between the years 1597 and 1599.[14] In the earlier period, the figures are placed on neutral background lit by a silvery color, their gestures are precise, mirroring the experimental spirit of the artist. The contours are delicate and sparing, the forms created are soft and unstressed and the colors pure. Neither the white nor the velvety black represent values of light or lack of light but are only concrete colors. The painting is homogenous with no suggestion of the expressive aspect. Chastel is of the opinion that already at this stage it is possible to sense an ambiguity resulting of the coexistence of both naïveté and innocence, on the one hand, and the awareness of translating content through a formal aspect, on the other hand; ambivalence that oscillates between a direct approach and an atmosphere of secrecy, between a pictorial inner balance and seemingly experimental elements.

Later, the works stress activity and deal with the figures as if they were to break through the margins of the painting. The background is darker and the rays of light are rigid though with powerful illumination. Special emphasis is given to the expression of drama and violence, obtained by the placement of the figures on the first plane of the painting, while the background seems to be "locked" by a wall of darkness, as if projecting them into the viewer's space. Chastel, then, discusses Caravaggio's formal development, stating that in later years the formal aspect is equivalent to content.

In *Calling of St. Matthew* (fig. 21) Bardon sees an additional formal turning-point, a highlighting technique based on forms as if appearing to break out of the background. This is done by means of a gradual and irregular brightening of the browns and blacks at the background, up to the emergence of the shape. Thus, the shape does not seem to have been placed upon the background, but more precisely, to be created out of it. This technique is Caravaggio's invention, weaving a new relativity between a colored shape and the foundation of the background. A relativity which is to be understood by means of the concepts of material per se, as texture, preparation of foundation, and color.[15] Her analysis of the work tries to show how formal aspects—as the highlighting technique—become the equivalent of content.

The event chosen by Caravaggio is the Calling of St. Matthew. Caravaggio chooses the moment of the calling, but combines it with the verses describing the other tax collectors and sinners. The meeting does not seem to take place in the Customs House but in an undefined place. In his painting, Caravaggio does not follow the literary description but combines time sequences while disregarding the space mentioned in the sources. He does not tell the story as known and deals with its essential symbolism.[16]

The usage of such symbolism might be the reason why Caravaggio places the earthly aspect on one side of the composition while the spiritual one is situated on the opposite side. A similar confrontation also exists in the treatment of the figures and their formal design. The earthly aspect depicts a group of five elegantly clad men sitting around a table on which coins are scattered. Matthew, sitting at the end of the table, is busy counting the money. The colors of the men's clothes are composed of different hues of red, mustard-yellow and blue, while the figure, whose back is turned to the viewer, is clothed in black and white. The painting's background features brown-black colors, pervading the hues of the socks, the figures' skin and the sub-hues of the colors. In front of the earthly unit are two standing figures: Jesus stands with a large part of his face turned towards the viewer, while Peter's back is enhanced. The colors chosen to depict the heavenly representatives are similar to the earthly ones, including reds, blacks, and even hues of yellow. However, the distribution of color is different, the colors have wider spaces, decoration and nuances are disregarded. Thus, the impression is given of whole, harmonic, "different" shapes. The spiritual value of Jesus and St. Peter is evident in spite of their being barefoot and wearing rags. They are shown as being taller than the earthly group and their moral authority is expressed by the gesture of Jesus' right hand thrust forward, as well as St. Peter's right hand, which is directed towards the same place and is a sort of enhancement. Resolutely raised, both hands condense the meaning of the calling.

Symbolism may be also attached to the design of the window. The only blind is open and through the opaque glass panes are perceived the brown-yellows of light-darkness, focusing in the "cross" formed by the frame. The left part of the window is closed. In addition to the emphasis of the cross, it seems that this light is not the source from which the figures are illuminated. The lighting or shadowing of the participants' faces does not depend on a defined physical source but on a source originating in the upper left end of the painting, where the spiritual group is depicted. Jesus and St. Peter, only partly illuminated, seem to emerge from the darkness. A sort of aura symbolized by a line of light coming out of the open part of the window may be a formal equivalent to the call to escape from the darkness of matter, from the opaque windows. The call to turn towards the spiritual light has no link to the physical source of blinding light pertaining to the material world in its external expression.

The depiction of the scene is not so clear and simple though. Caravaggio places the heavenly on the left and the earthly on the right, contrary to traditional iconography. The heavenly representatives break out of darkness, poorly lighted in comparison to the sitting figures. The light out of the window is opaque and does not promise anything. Therefore, the representatives of spirituality appear bearing a message, but it is a message connected to inflexibility and religious coercion.

Bardon writes in length about the situation of the Catholic Church in Caravaggio's times. The Church's main goal was to fight the Reformation. The economic and social situation did not contribute to the general atmosphere and the gap between the social strata affected a large part of the population. The Church ruled not by means of persuasion but by coercion, enabling the cruel Inquisition. This period of extreme and conflicting atmosphere left no place to challenge the religious ethos accepted by convention, a period in which Galileo Galilei and Giordano Bruno were persecuted because, in opposition to the Aristotelian approach favored by the Church, they stated that the Earth rotates around its own axis and the sun. Galileo chose to retract publicly, although privately continued to insist that "eppur si mouve," but Bruno, who did not retract, was burned at the stake.

Side by side with fanaticism and compulsion, the Humanists circles, as well as reduced circles pertaining to the Church institutions, revealed a great interest in the alternative way of thinking represented by Galileo Galilei and Giordano Bruno. Cardinal Del Monte, Caravaggio's protector, defended Galilei and enabled him to teach at Padova and Pisa. Bardon believes that the spirit of the period doubtlessly infiltrated Caravaggio's thought and perception. Avoiding mentioning any direct influences, she states that the double meaning expressed in Caravaggio's creations might derive from his dangerous movement between a-priori religious, dogmatic way of thinking, and that based on a-posteriori empiric thought.[17]

The ambivalent formal design which I have discussed in connection with *The Calling of St. Matthew* may or may not express the spirit of the period, as neither the presentation nor the artist's intentions are sufficiently clear: would the spiritual representatives bring forth salvation, or would they cause doom and darkness? By using formal equivalents, Caravaggio expresses his feelings despite the period's upheavals.

I turn now to *The Conversion of St. Paul* (fig. 22). The story is mentioned in *The Acts of the Apostles*. According to the Scriptures, Saul the soldier was suddenly thrown to the earth, blinded by a heavenly light, hearing the voice of the Lord. Friedlaender mentions some examples of paintings depicting the subject.[18] Among them are Raphael's (fig. 23), Michelangelo's (fig. 24), and Zuccari's (fig. 25), which show the actual falling, the frightened horse, the heavenly revelation and the tumult arisen amongst the soldiers. The artists mentioned want to provide a concretization of the divine and describe the Lord accompanied at times by angels. Many later artists, like Signorelli and Pordenone, give up the concrete description of the Lord and his entourage depicting only a source of light. Artists such as Moreto and Parmigianino go a step further and dispense with the description of the Lord and the source of light altogether, choosing to describe only the frightened horse and its rider fallen on the earth, partly lying, head upturned and body tense. Thus, these artists want to express the saint listening to the words of the Lord.

The later, 1601 version of Caravaggio's *Conversion of St. Paul*, also known as *Conversion on the Way to Damascus* (fig. 26) is different from the version he painted a year earlier (fig. 22)[19] and from any other previous versions. The composition contains three main figures: Paul, his horse and the horse-groom. As in *The Cardsharps* also in this case, the viewer is looking at the scene at close quarters—the figures concentrated in a narrow space. These two facts enhance the tension and the viewer's involvement.[20]

As opposed to his antecessors, Caravaggio does not depict the moment of the fall but the state of things thereafter: St. Paul's weakness and inability of movement (fig. 27).[21] The young, robust soldier lies on the ground, his back glued to the earth, the legs spread and knees somewhat risen, the arms open and also risen, as if asking to identify or hold onto something. Maybe the hands are widely open in order to refuse what is happening to him. The tension created derives from the soldier's fall from the horse and his helplessness. Similarly to Goliath and Holofernes, the drama is awakened by the fall of the powerful. Those who were considered heroes are unable to react, as mere objects. Moreover, the painting lacks any hint of heavenly sights, sources of light, or an attentive saint. Caravaggio's

Paul lies on his back, while the horse and groom shield him.

In comparison to horses depicted in previous paintings, this horse is not drawn as a noble war animal, and the horse-groom is not one of the accompanying soldiers (fig. 28). It is evident that the giant horse, which occupies the main part of the composition, is a labor beast, the leaning groom is a peasant acquainted with daily toil. In this painting, man and beast lack the qualities of nobility traditionally accorded. They stand vertically to the fallen figure and look as if they were in control of the situation, lacking the excitement and fright overwhelming Paul. They may not be aware of the events and their transcendence. The horse looks at its rider kindly, curiously and with possible indifference. Instead of rushing to help the fallen man, the horse-groom is busy removing the horse's bridle.

Saul-Paul, elegant in red attire, wears a helmet decorated with a feather, his shield and sword thrust on the ground, the body powerless and all his belongings scattered around, useless. The depiction of the saint as weak and deprived of any transcendental light is a subject of controversy among scholars. Friedlaender compares Michelangelo's and Caravaggio's approach, asserting that the latter deals with the "seen," the concrete, and the earthier. In his words, Caravaggio does not deal with the "*idea fantastica*" but with a flesh-and-blood horse, a labor animal lacking noble attributes.[22] The use of the concrete and the natural are opposed in their character to classical idealization and to mannerist abstraction. However, he claims that this depiction should not be referred to as lacking religious feelings; an absence of a physical source of light, as well as the artificial illumination of the figures point to "magic realism" and "magic light"[23] that enhance the psychological and dramatic dimension. Paul is described as if experiencing the beginnings of an ecstatic process, which will lead to the conversion itself.

In contrast to Raphael's or other painters' creations, the saint has closed eyes as if the miracle takes place beyond what is seen. Friedlaender believes that Caravaggio may be less intellectual and less symbolic than the preceding painters, but his approach to the miracle is more direct and natural. Paul's arms and hands are held yearningly upwards as if wishing to hug the voice of God. This posture means that the saint witnessed a great sight, and out of fear mixed with joy, he responds to the powerful voice that penetrated his soul and body. Friedlaender opposes other scholars explaining the strange posture of the fall in Caravaggio's work as an epilepsy attack. In his opinion, this depiction should not be regarded as trying to trace a pathological case, but to stress the psychological drama—drama created by the consent of a stubborn, Christianity-loathing soldier, to become an apostle of Christ.[24] Janson expresses a similar view. Precisely the lack of theological dogma and the direct approach to the miracle awakened the sympathy of Catholics and Protestants alike, who did not have to be learned in order to relate to the feeling of the experience.[25]

Unlike these scholars, who do not discuss the contextual implications resulting of the deviation in style and traditional presentation, others, like Hauser, believe that precisely this deviation caused the gap between Caravaggio and the Church.[26] More moderate than Hauser, Gombrich discusses the different in Caravaggio's work, the inability of his contemporaries to comprehend him, and his decisive influence on the future development of art.[27]

Chastel expresses the same ideas directly and unambiguously. He believes that the artist wishes to embarrass the traditional ethos presenting a subject traditionally considered transcendent in a lesser way, thus implementing a lay approach towards life and religion.[28]

Bardon, who does not usually express such direct opinions, presents matters in Chastel's way, and goes even further. Her suggestions may be interpreted as existentialist, as she believes that Caravaggio indeed challenged the established and dogmatic tradition. For this artist there is only one reality shared by the fallen soldier, the horse-groom and the horse. Furthermore, Bardon advances an interesting idea. Paul, and indirectly the artist himself, fall appalled by the unknown: the incomprehensible is the main subject of the painting. Paul has nothing left to hold as darkness of sight has fallen upon him; he neither sees nor understands anything. The question arises whether the horse sees anything, and if anyone is aware of the event. Bardon sustains that if God actually exists, he must be part of matter, and therefore ungraspable and non-immediate. Thus, Bardon wonders whether Caravaggio paints inability to know and lack of faith. Bardon is not decisive, and chooses to leave this matter unresolved.[29]

The scholars mentioned above—in spite of the differences between their opinions—reveal a positive, supporting approach to Caravaggio's work. However, Berenson, whose conservative criticism belongs to the aesthetics patterns of the nineteenth century, is the only one of Caravaggio's critics who accuses him of malicious painting and bad intentions, and does not find any justification for the figures populating this work, such as the "the dumb beast," referring to the horse, or "the plumed and majestic patriarch"—that is Caravaggio's alternate depiction of what should be, in Berenson's opinion, a young and alert horse-groom. In his view, "incongruity, at times malicious incongruity, henceforth dominated Caravaggio's work in Rome."[30]

Caravaggio's work indeed raises several questions. Does Caravaggio really have a natural and religious approach to the miracles phenomenon, and displays a deep religious feeling, or does he rebel against the foundations of tradition and describes the idea of the incapacity of knowledge? Moreover, is he willfully misleading, his whole intention being to enrage his viewers? The contextual ambivalence I have dealt with while discussing *The Calling of St. Matthew* and *Judith Beheading Holofernes* repeats itself in this case: it is as if it were impossible to properly understand at whose side Caravaggio stands—the perpetrator or the victim? And, as if it were impossible to understand if the figure of Jesus in *The Calling of St.*

Matthew stands for hope and salvation or utter pessimism. Here again there is a difference of opinion regarding a display of religiosity on the artist's part, or precisely the contrary: being a challenge to the general pattern and the accepted religious ethos.

The ambivalence of the content is conveyed through the plastic treatment which conceals in its form a variety of possibilities and ways of comprehension. In his book, *Art and Psychoanalysis*, Peter Fuller surveys the interpretation of the concept of Expressionism. In his view, Alberti states in the fifteenth century that *expresia* is a field which must be included in the artist's knowledge.[31] The reason for it is that a painting of good quality influences the state of mind of the viewer who responds to the expressed feelings. Therefore, the artist must know how to convey feelings through appropriate painterly postures or expressions.[32] Alberti's *expresia* was in effect until the nineteenth century. But, in the twentieth century there was a change in the perception of the concept, and its new meaning focused on the ability of the artist to express subjective feelings through colors and shapes. The figurative basis is still in effect, but it became a sort of pictorial tool containing the invisible body of the artist. In other words, if until the end of the nineteenth century perception was focused on the external aspect of the figures—namely, an aspect that was generally accepted, at the end of the nineteenth century and the beginning of the twentieth century, colors and shapes do not derive anymore from a direct perception of reality but originate more and more in the unique, subjective inner being of the creator.

As mentioned, Bardon expresses a similar idea when referring explicitly to Caravaggio. In her view, the search for formal abstract schemes is a need of Caravaggio's because he does not accept the literary a-priori concerning his painting.[33] In order to create a kind of new acquaintance with reality through painting, the artist must go through abstraction to invent an iconography in which the meaning is not separated from the form itself. Gash believes as well that Caravaggio's success as originator and creator of images is rooted in his ability to accord renewed vitality and validity to traditional images due to his great sensitivity, expressed in the presentation of themes and his interest in human nature.[34]

The deviation from tradition in the presentation of subjects, dealt with in the chapter on realism, and the introduction of the personal dimension, presented in the chapter on the self in Caravaggio's creation, ultimately find their unequivocal expression in the plastic and artistic language of unprecedented Caravaggioism.

Rejection of Religious Dogma

This chapter, discussing the fourth criterion, religion as a domain freed from dogma and a field in which personal thought is imbibed, is linked to modernism as well. Religion understood as such is anchored in a subjective state of mind. Freedom of collective dogma means a choice of a personal iconography decoded solely by the thorough knowledge of a particular artist.[1]

Analyzing the theme of death in the nineteenth century, Nochlin makes it clear that in contrast to previous tradition, realism treats death, as well as religion, empirically with no transcendent significance.[2] In contrast to El Greco's painting *El Entierro del Conde de Orgaz (The Burial of the Count of Orgaz)*—brought as an example to represent the traditional which links the earthly with the heavenly—realism intends to depict what is captured by the senses and gives up any supernatural presence in art. Religious ceremonies are, therefore, described by realism as being social happenings. The empiric basis serves as a starting point to deal with religious issues, as well as with specific subjects like the death of Jesus. Approaching transcendental contents with an earthly and empirical thought is, according to Nochlin, a significant turning-point. The Judeo-Christian tradition serves to emphasize this turning-point, for it believes that earthy phenomena are linked to the divine; the virtuous will be rewarded, while the wrongdoer will be punished. The descriptions of Heaven versus the horrors of Hell are visual demonstrations to exemplify the idea of reward and punishment. Death, therefore, is considered as a mere passage in an ampler circle of life. Earthly life serves as a stage, which will determine future resurrection or final death. The belief in resurrection colors the act of death with optimistic and noble nuances, for this state is but a passage to a higher life.

In contrast to this view, nineteenth-century Realism swerves from any sort of interpretation which is not entirely empirical. Every religious description will now be absent of divine or supernatural characteristics. The death of Christ or of a saint will be accurately depicted as if they were mere human beings; down-to-earth beings that fear the physical final annihilation, the unknown, or the presumption that beyond life they might await an obscure, meaningless emptiness, devouring the physical body, leaving behind only tormenting nothingness. Every religious scene is interpreted into an earthy language and is described as a concrete occurrence.

In this respect, I consider in this chapter Caravaggio's relation and approach to religion more closely and endeavor to position the artist as the first realist foreseeing nineteenth-century Realism. From the pure iconographical point of view, Caravaggio adapts the traditional and conventional symbols, however his way of painting—composition, figures, usage of light and shadow, mode of representation of the subject—all these show a comprehension which violates the existing conventions: saints are painted as common people; the death of the Virgin is demonstrated as the death of a mortal human; while angels look as if they were tempting youths whose artificial wings do not seem to be a natural part of their bodies. An upheaval occurs here regarding the traditional description of the figures. A similar upheaval occurs relating to iconography. There is a blurring confusion between the victim who is sacrificed and the one who commits the crime. A blur necessarily poses the question whether the aggressor and the victim are but one sole and inseparable being.

I begin by discussing the image of the saint in Caravaggio's work and conclude on the image of Mary specifically. Even though I have, here and there, touched upon these themes in previous chapters, I wholly focus on them in this one, returning to previously discussed works and suggesting others that depict holy figures. By also comparing these to other similar works by Caravaggio's contemporaries and predecessors, I try to stress his unique solemnly reticent treatment of these characters and their almost existential atmosphere.

THE IMAGE OF THE SAINT

Caravaggio's revolutionary thinking materializes even in his approach to the image of the saint. At first sight, it seems that there is no deviation from tradition, but a further, deeper inspection reveals the way in which the subject and the images are presented, and it raises questions about the approach of this enigmatic artist.

The two versions of St. Matthew and the Angel (figs. 29 and 30) enable me to open the discussion. According to tradition, St. Matthew is the writer of the first Book of the New Testament. Traditional iconography calls for presenting him accompanied by his symbol, an angel, and depicted as a writer guided by the angel while writing the Gospel.[3] Caravaggio is faithful to the long standing tradition (see first version; fig. 29). However, the unique depiction might lend another meaning to the situation. The composition includes only two persons—the non-haloed Matthew is shown frontally, sitting on a chair, and turning towards the angel standing at his left. The figure chosen by Caravaggio as the saint is a peasant, barefooted, wearing rags, with a strenuous expression caused by the effort of writing, which seems unusual to him. The inkpot needed for writing is absent from the painting since there is no table to put it on. The book lies on the saint's crossed legs, turning them into a support for the book.

The angel at his left is shown frontally. In opposition to the coarseness of St. Matthew, the angel is youthful, mischievous and ostentatious. His stature equals the seating saint. The big white wings look as artificial attachments, due to the difference between their light color in comparison to his darker body. The brightness of the wings lightens part of his face. The hand lightly touches St. Matthew's and seemingly guides his writing. It appears as if St. Matthew cannot act alone. His clumsy feet are very close to the boyish angel whose leg bursts into the field of man. This physical proximity necessarily cancels the hierarchy between the earthly element and the heavenly one.

The presentation of St. Matthew as a dependent, chance performer of directions given by a seducing physical angel apparently caused the clergy of the San Luigi dei Francesi Church to reject the work. Indeed, according to the testimony of Bellori: "After he had finished the central picture of St. Matthew and installed it on the altar, the priests took it down, saying that the figure with its legs crossed and its feet rudely exposed to the public had neither decorum nor the appearance of a saint."[4] Baglione suggests indirectly the tumult caused by this work of Caravaggio:

> When Federico Zuccaro came to see this picture, while I was there, he exclaimed: "What is all the fuss about? [...] I do not see anything here other than the style of Giorgione in the picture of the saint when Christ calls him to the Apostolate;" and sneering, astonished by such commotion, he turned his back and left.[5]

The latter version (fig. 30) may explain why the first one promoted such opposition among the clergy, to the extent of being rejected. In the second version, known as well as *The Inspiration of St. Matthew*, the saint appears writing the Gospel, and holding the pen with confident fingers. The book lies on a desk, his foot resting on a stool. The haloed saint is of noble intelligent features, capable of comprehending the Gospel. Here the angel hovers over the man with no physical contact. The saint is extremely alert, with his right leg firm on earth and the left on the stool. His bare feet are partly shadowed. Although following dogma, Caravaggio still imprints his personal seal: the boyish angel here too emerges from darkness with no visible wings. The guiding is transmitted by hand signs, which might not be entirely captured.

Bardon concludes that the inability of these two worlds to meet is reflected in the composition of the painting. She points out the round contour of St. Matthew in opposition to the angel's contour, while each of the figures forms an independent, separate spatial unit, the arms forming an inward movement.[6] Caravaggio's approach is opposed to the Catholic faith. The difficulty of communication between angel and man symbolizes the insurmountable gap between the divine and the human. Here too one encounters the ambivalence existent in previously discussed works: one never knows Caravaggio's secret heart tendency.[7]

Kitson stresses that the themes might seem simple and clear at first glance but the ambiance is secretive.[8] Along the same lines, Chastel maintains that there is a problematic link between form and symbol.[9] It seems that the non-clarity between virtue and vice, as understood by convention, constitutes in Caravaggio's work a source of numerous questions, which have remained unanswered till the day.

In *The Martyrdom of St. Matthew* the moment before the killing is portrayed (fig. 31). According to tradition, this saint converted Hirtacus, King of Ethiopia, but was killed by him, as the saint refused to grant him permission to marry a second wife, the virgin Iphigenia.[10] Similarly to *Conversion on the Way to Damascus*, in which the saint is shown at his utmost impotence after the fall, utterly subject to destiny,[11] here, too, Caravaggio does not choose the moment of the killing, ending all anxieties, but prefers to depict the instant gathering anxiety at the climax.

This climax is enhanced by the painted figures, witnessing the event, much like the viewers. The figures are placed on the right of the painting, on its left and in the first plane. The figure on the right, with the back to the viewer, has been cut off and is evidently recoiling from the impact of the scene. The figure on the left, closer to the spectator, holds the ground as a last recourse and an outlet of tension. The movements and expressions of the figures manifest the outburst of emotions and their involvement; the boy on the right is looking at the scene from above, his body is turning as if to run out of the picture; some of the figures express their commotion lifting hands or watching the scene and seeking refuge inwards.

According to certain scholars, some of the recoiling figures recall the self-portrait of the artist. Gash believes that the image of the bearded king, on the left, showing only the head and a small part of the body, is Caravaggio's self-portrait.[12] Friedlaender, on the other hand, finds the figure at the back, with only the lighted head shown and turning sadly to the right, to be that of a self-portrait.[13] Whichever figure may or may not be the artist's actual portrait, it is possible to find traits common to both figures as introspection, resignation, and the impotence to cope with or to reject a cruel destiny. The destiny is concretized, in this case, in the figure of the killer who becomes the center and axis of the painting. Indeed, the figure of the killer is illuminated and most precisely detailed. This figure is portrayed as a handsome youngster, whose solid, muscular body is clearly stressed. The beauty of the killer is evident even in the mane of curls adorned by a ribbon. This "Greek god" is holding a sword in his right hand while grabbing the right arm of the fallen saint with his left one. The body of the victim lies impotently at the feet of this unique, chivalrous killer.

Victim and aggressor are illuminated, and the clarity is strongly stressed by the threatening darkness lurking below. It looks as if the saint were lying on the brink of an enormous black precipice, while his left hand is already turning down, towards the darkness. A cross-like shape is created by the open arms, vertical to the width of the painting, and by the body, lying parallel to its width. This cross, made of the members of a person, probably serves as the earthly echo of the shining cross above him, bursting out of a cloud. Above this cloud the boyish angel bends, turning towards the saint, his head foreshortened, holding in his right hand a palm, symbol of the triumph of Christianity over death.[14] The palm is directed and offered to the open, expecting hand of the saint, but the base of the hand is decisively clasped in the hand of the culprit. This great drama receives further meaning due to the triumphal palm, physically close, but far from saving St. Matthew from a certain death, so palpable and real.

The composition of the painting stresses the feeling of plunging into perdition and death. The heads create a continuity of falling heights which begin their way down at the angel positioned in the upper part of the painting and end at the fallen image of the saint. The form of a triangle is thus created: the basis—the saint's body; a vertical—the killer; and the diagonal—the arms of both aggressor and sacrificed; this is a vicious triangle capturing within the essence of killer and victim. In this context, it is possible to understand why the candle of faith, placed above the head of the aggressor, produces a particularly subdued, isolated light, in view of the human deeds being performed below.

The revolutionary approach of Caravaggio, openly contradicting the tradition by stressing the aggressor instead of the victim is further exemplified by comparing Caravaggio's St. Matthew and St. Paul with *The Martyrdom of St. Sebastian* by Pollaiuolo (fig. 32).[15] Pollaiuolo uses the triangular format, but it is an isosceles triangle, with the saint on its apex and the killers aiming their arrows from below. In this case, the body and face of St. Sebastian are handsome. Virtues and sanctity are reflected in the idealized portraying of the saint compared to his murderers, who look as typical earthy characters, devoid of any individual, unique characterization. The structure of this work by Pollaiuolo is in accordance with the Catholic hierarchy, which places Virtue above, and in the central axis of the composition.[16]

In the later version of the St. Paul painting discussed earlier (fig. 26),[17] Caravaggio seems to have turned things upside-down and not in vain: St. Paul is lying, dominated by a horse and a horse-groom who are indifferent to the event. In the St. Matthew painting, the saint is so close to redemption, and it is precisely this closeness which enhances the feeling of perdition of the restrained figure, portrayed as if it were at the bottom of the scale, in the downward proclivity of the figures. Again, the artist retrieves the idea of depiction from tradition, although by means of his unique approach, he suggests a different meaning to his work.

This meaning will be even better understood, by comparing this work to Barocci's painting on the subject of martyrdom but that of St. Vitale (fig. 33). Barocci has depicted the saint lying on the ground, overpowered by the killer. Both are equally illuminated, unlike the shadowed figures surrounding them. The angel, shown hovering above, is a heavenly creature, maybe symbolizing redemption. Barocci does not place the angel close to humans and separates the higher and lower realms. The closeness and elimination of boundaries in Caravaggio's work may enhance the lack of a possibility of redemption, despite the accessibility of the angel.

In the vein of the two previous works discussed in this chapter, Caravaggio chooses the most difficult moment for his *Crucifixion of St. Peter* (fig. 34) as well. The saint is depicted tied and nailed to the cross along with his three executioners. The crucifixion has already been completed, leaving only the elevation of the instrument of death. Three anonymous figures carry out the sentence by means of hard, strenuous physical work. One of the perpetrators is depicted as bending under the weight of the cross, his back turned to the viewer, his bare feet stained with mud. This figure has a visual continuation in the form of another bent perpetrator seen from behind, pulling a rope. The two figures form a diagonal. A second diagonal is formed by the two other figures, the saint and the executioner, positioned as the continuation of the legs pertaining to the saint fastened upside down. Both diagonals create a living cross. Again, Caravaggio creates a parallel between the shape of the wooden cross carrying the victim and the shape of the cross originated by human figures.[18]

The executioners have no particular traits. Two of them are seen from behind and the face of the third one is shadowed. They are busy with their task, while the saint is almost completely illuminated, staring out of the space of the painting, as if perplexed, or subjecting himself to destiny. Bardon discusses the paradox of the crucifixion as a way to achieve salvation. In her view, neither of the persons taking part in the event is aware of the meaning of the crucifixion;[19] actually, they lack eyes or mouth. There is an uneasy feeling that suffering must be endured in order to attain a triumph which has not been promised at all. Moreover, the executioners themselves are made to do something without understanding its purpose. They act out of ignorance, being a product of the material reality, as everything else.

The difference in Caravaggio's perception will be better comprehended by comparison to Michelangelo's *Crucifixion of St. Peter* (fig. 35) and to the later painter José de Ribera's *Martyrdom of Saint Bartholomew* (fig. 36). Hibbard stresses the contribution of Michelangelo's revolutionary perception to the artists that followed him, as the cross is shown in the process of being hoisted, the saint looking at the space outside the margins of the painting, rebellious and accusing.[20] Caravaggio borrows two main motifs from Michelangelo: the raising of the cross and the look of the saint, aimed at the outside of the painting. But, as usual, his approach entails diverse meanings. The details of landscape appearing in the former painting are removed, and instead only a handful of details are left, as the triangle of ground and some rocks in the lower part of the painting. The large crowd assembled in Michelangelo's work, witnessing and taking part in the great sorrow has also disappeared.

Caravaggio maintains the victim and the three executioners, faithfully carrying out their task. The loneliness of the victim is so moving because he lacks a partner to his terrible fate. As in the *St. Matthew*, the physical proximity enhances the absence and irony of the upheavals of destiny. All the figures, without exception, co-operate in the act of crucifixion. They are all part of the same vicious circle, united in being subjugated to an incomprehensible and irrational circumstantial compulsion.

The Spanish painter Ribera, who takes from Caravaggio the bases of the formal painting, follows in spirit and perception the approach of Michelangelo. He portrays landscape—albeit not very conspicuously—and in his work appears also the congregation expressing horror and sorrow as a reaction to the tragic event.[21] The use made of *chiaroscuro* might indicate certain daylight hours, as opposed to Caravaggio's *chiaroscuro*, which is not the result of real illumination: the lightening is artificial and of psychological value. All figures are more or less equally illuminated, but they all emerge out of darkness, while only the crucified saint is about to return to the threatening shadows bursting in from below.[22]

The melancholy and the lack of faith in redemption, which came upon St. Paul while embracing the void at the time of his conversion, likewise overwhelm St. Matthew. The latter extends a hand hoping for an impossible redemption—at least, in the immediate world. The same are to be found in the image of St. Peter, who has been left alone, confronting his fate, while his abusers enhance his existential loneliness. The melancholy and lack of faith feature also in works depicting Mary, the Holy Virgin, to which I shall turn now.

THE IMAGE OF MARY

In *Rest on the Flight to Egypt* (fig. 37) the Holy Family is portrayed in the open, while a youthful, coquettish angel shown from the back plays his violin for the listeners. The composition is divided in two parts, the angel marking the center of the painting. Joseph sits on the left, with bundles and a wineskin appearing below. The ass behind Joseph looks at the scene. Joseph and the ass listen to the sound of music. Joseph even holds the notes for the angel. As in Caravaggio's previous works, the angel is youthfully depicted. He is delicate, with a feminine poise, his cloth exposes shapely, tempting legs. The angel and his listeners are immersed in their occupation, paying no heed to their surroundings.

On the right of the painting, the Mother of God is drawn according to the "Madonna of Humility" tradition. Unlike Joseph, who chooses to settle on the bundles, Mary sits on the ground. She is disconnected from the wonderful reality around her, expressed in a beautiful lyric landscape.[23] She holds her sleeping son with the left hand, while the right hand is limp and lax, the head resting on her baby's. Has she fallen asleep? An atmosphere of sadness envelops the lonely figure. The open spaces left by the artist as background to Mary's image, unlike the closure of the background behind the other figures, enhance the drama. It looks as if Mary is not aware of the beauty of nature or the grace of the angel. She does not hear the sounds, being entirely withdrawn. Her body is slack following the vicissitudes of the way, her soul tired of the hardships of life.

As usual, Caravaggio enhances the drama by presenting opposing poles. As in *The Crucifixion of St. Peter*, here, too, Mary's loneliness becomes insufferable, enhanced by the presence of the other figures. The closeness of the surrounding people does not ease nor lessen her pain or misfortune.

The solitude is better comprehended by comparing this work with Tintoretto's *Flight into Egypt* (fig. 38).[24] Unlike Caravaggio's,

Mary by Tintoretto rides an ass, as if it was a noble horse. She is alert, gazing lovingly at her son, her head haloed.[25] Joseph leads the ass, looking backwards, checking the valuable human load. The ass seems to understand Joseph's look and lowers its head. Tintoretto follows the traditional iconography and assigns Mary great importance, according to the appropriate hierarchy, whereas Caravaggio's Mary is smaller, as if placed in the rear plane of the picture, while Joseph and the angel are dominant.

The loneliness of the Holy Mother is concretized also in Caravaggio's *Adoration by the Shepherds* (also called *Nativity*; fig. 39). Here the Virgin is lying on miserable straw bedding in a poor shed. She feebly leans on the manger, holding her newborn baby. As in the previous painting, her eyes are closed, the face grieved, foreboding the future. Leaning towards her the worshipping shepherds create a sort of lighted diagonal, shining upon the dark background created by the body of the ass and the woody material of the shed. Similarly to the music of the angel's violin in *Rest on the Flight to Egypt* the shepherds do not touch her impenetrable soul. The sincere worshipping and adoration of the shepherds are not responded and Mary remains withdrawn.

The painting *Madonna of Loreto* or *Madonna of the Pilgrims* (fig. 40) recaptures the legend according to which the house of Mary and Joseph was moved first from Nazareth to Dalmatia, and finally placed in Loreto by the angels. Loreto was chosen after the invasion of the Holy Land by the Moslems and the consequent expulsion of the crusaders.[26] The Loreto house became a place of pilgrimage. The main focus of attention was a wooden statue of the Madonna. Barefoot pilgrims came from afar to worship it. They believed that the statue became alive a number of times.[27] Friedlaender claims that the "slightly archaic character" of Caravaggio's Madonna derives from the artist's intention to restore the old statue of Mary, acting as mediator between God and mortals, as well as fulfilling the aspirations of the pilgrims.[28]

However, Caravaggio's Madonna has characteristics reminding Parmigianino's *Madonna of the Long Neck* (fig. 41), both being delicate and graceful, holding big sized babies in their arms. Caravaggio's Madonna stands one foot placed over the other, her posture utterly relaxed. She lowers her gaze towards two crutched figures of old worshippers, her body unapproachable. Here, also, the physical closeness to the Mother of God does not bridge between the divine and the human. The Madonna stands on the threshold of a high door, and the pilgrims stay out of frame, their staffs serving as a natural barrier in between. Bardon claims that the separation between the divine and the human is stressed by the pilgrims' staffs, rebutting the figures and creating a gap between mortals and the inaccessible saintly mother.[29] Mary holds her son as if trying to distance him from the earthly world. Much like in previously discussed works, this Madonna, too, is isolated in her pain and grief, facing her misfortune, estranged and unattainable.

As seen, the feeling of hesitation and lack of faith in a possible redemption characterize Caravaggio's saintly figures. Caravaggio's existential approach might have instigated scholars as Kitson to question Caravaggio's religiosity. According to him, the *chiaroscuro* characterizing Caravaggio's work has an ethical and iconographic meaning: the *chiaroscuro* does not unite but separates, serving as a reflection of a degraded sublime sphere.[30] Darkness and aura symbolize a complex world, in which vice and virtue are intermingled. Contemplating the artist's works, one can assume that the physical and spiritual darkness are preponderant. If redemption or clarity is present, they remain unattainable, stressing the presence of existential darkness.

Summary

This book is based on four criteria intended to define the essence of the concept "modernism" and is accordingly divided into four chapters in order to demonstrate how the criteria I have discussed in each one apply to Caravaggio's works. Regarding each criteria yet again, I now discuss, as a form of summary, the formal, iconographic, aesthetic, and finally, philosophic implications of Caravaggio's work.

On realism

All along this book, I have tried to show that Caravaggio's realism is based on his personal, unconventional approach, embodying the unique perception of this artist. The artist does not shun the use of any motif derived from reality in a unique, unconventional way, as content or formal language. Even sixteenth-century scholars were aware of his uniqueness. Carel van Mander (1528–1606) stresses Caravaggio's faithfulness to nature, adding that any type of art, which is not based on life itself, is nothing but a jest, a childish game. He maintains that even if a painting is perfect, it will never be as good as that which is faithful to nature.[1] Van Mander does not dwell on the difference between the Renaissance perception of reality and Caravaggio's unique perception of it, but he points out this artist's distinction.

Modern scholars, like Hibbard and Janson, are aware of such differences between Caravaggio and his predecessors. Hibbard, for instance, mentions the uniqueness of Caravaggesque realism, precisely in his deviation from the Renaissance and the refusal to be subject to the idealistic theories prevailing in his time.[2] Caravaggio does not subject himself to a-priori theories, as van Mander does make clear,[3] but relies on his own perception. Janson differentiates between the Renaissance comprehension of reality, based on a collective view, and Caravaggio's, based on his subjective view, suggesting that his work should be called "naturalism," not "realism," as Caravaggio paints figures of saints as if he were painting common people.[4]

Kitson points out the essential difference between Caravaggio and his predecessors convinced that deviating from past traditions turns him into the first anti-academy artist, a great revolutionary that sacrificed beauty on the altar of truth.[5] Indeed, Kitson refers to Renaissance beauty, based on restrain, harmony, inner balance, the idealization of figures, and their place in the composition according to a hierarchy of importance, while Caravaggio ignores these values, sacrificing them for the sake of his subjective truth. Thus, his realism reflects his personality. Kitson stresses these facts through the analysis of the figures in Caravaggio's works. He distinguishes between two main periods: the early period, when the artist designs his figures naturalistically and the later period, when he does not choose nature as a source, turning instead to what Kitson calls the "realms of imagination and invention"[6]—namely, the inner world of the artist. This turning-point, leading to a neglect of the imitation of nature and a rapprochement to the self—where the seeds for imagination and invention are to be found—is what causes Kitson to perceive Caravaggio as a fully-fledged modern artist.

ON THE SELF AND ON FORMAL EQUIVALENTS

The discussion of the works demonstrated how the subjective view marked by the artist's personality is translated into formal equivalents. Francesco Scannelli (1616–1663) states, as early as the seventeenth century, that Caravaggio's approach to reality reflects his own personality, which is also expressed by the use of plastic means extraneous to conventional painting.[7] Scannelli believes that this artist introduces his inner world into his paintings, expressing it through innovative artistic means. However, Scannelli lacks historical perspective, and is unable to accept as virtuous the deviation from the accepted norms in Caravaggio's work. Therefore, he maintains that the paintings are not complete, lacking grace, architecture, perspective, dignity, or any other significant elements used by the great masters.[8]

Hibbard, a contemporary scholar who has a proper historical perspective, arrives to a similar conclusion regarding Caravaggio's unusual plastic expression. Although not as Scannelli, Hibbard sees as virtuous the artist's refusal to accommodate the idealist theories of his time.[9] Gash links the ends and connects between objective reality and reality as perceived and marked by the self and the synthesis of these two realities as eventually reflected in what I have called Caravaggio's formal equivalents.[10]

Caravaggio's creation and the formal equivalents that reflect his own perception of matters are extraneous to the period, as above mentioned. However, these are the characteristics on which a large part of late-nineteenth-century and the beginnings of twentieth-century Symbolism will be based. In his book, *ABC de la peinture*, Denis explains the twofold nature of formal equivalents. The first deals with formal values as a two-dimensional surface is covered by colors that are united in a certain order. The second refers to the intention, that is, not to copy but to translate nature; to bring forth an anti-naturalism which is a synthesis of feelings and composition.[11]

Denis clarifies that instead of an idea of nature as perceived through temperament, he opts for an idea of nature as an equivalent or symbol, that is, feelings or states of mind aroused by a certain sight. The artist's imagination creates plastic equivalents capable to reproduce the same feelings or states of mind without necessarily copying the original sight. Each emotional affinity finds an objective harmony which serves as a mirror.[12]

Gash expresses the same ideas when referring to Caravaggio's work, without specifically using the term "formal equivalents:" "In wedding imaginative design to realistically observed detail [the artist] was not only better able to illuminate meaning, but also actually extended tradition by creating a new and immaculate balance between the two Renaissance objectives of imitating nature and perfecting style."[13]

The contemporary painter, Frank Stella,[14] says that in his unique way Caravaggio succeeds in inventing a new atmosphere of "rounding" space and having it extend towards the viewer. Caravaggio also grants his figures a feeling of presence and real activity. Caravaggio's figures are more human, approachable, as if designed by the canvas itself, which emphasizes the pictorial drama, creating an almost tangible illusion.[15] For Stella, all of this is revolutionary; he sees in Caravaggio a forbearer of Modern art,[16] while other Renaissance painters only accomplished an illusion, a perception of space by means of an invisible window.

Stella accounts that after seeing Caravaggio's *St. John the Baptist* (fig. 42)[17] he comprehended the affinity existent between the masters' works and abstraction. He understood the singularity and greatness of this painting as it could be reformulated in abstract, for elemental characteristics could serve both figurative and abstract art. The activity of the painterly aspects and of the figures takes place in a virtual space. A space surrounds the figures and is present likewise in front or behind things. This fact transfers a feeling that things are not cramped, but that they leave a virtual open space behind.

ON RELIGION

Similarly to the three previous criteria, the religious approach deals with personal observation and uncommon interpretation. However, the scholars' points of view are frequently opposed and even contradictory on this matter. According to Friedlaender, in *Conversion on the way to Damascus* (fig. 22) Caravaggio wishes to turn the miracle into an easily perceived event in order to bring the miracle phenomenon closer to the spirit of the people. Caravaggio's approach is more natural and direct when compared to the painters that preceded him.[18] Friedlaender believes that Caravaggio is less an intellectual and a symbolist than his predecessors, but this fact does not contradict his religiosity. On the contrary, continues Friedlaender, as Caravaggio experiences religion naturally and directly, his motifs are less symbolic and more direct, connecting his faith to the severe religious atmosphere of his time.[19]

Bardon raises the question on Caravaggio's religious attitude. Time and again she leads the reader to conclude on the great uncertainty of Caravaggio's religiosity, without conclusively stating it. When describing *Entombment* (fig. 43), she states that "la grande roue de la fatalité humaine tourne dans le néant."[20] Later on, matters are clarified: "The angle of the stone and the blackness of the earth cut by it are placed at the viewer's eye-level. Thus, the viewer, as the painted bearer of the body, feels the absolute disintegration of the world, after the death of Jesus, with no salvation possible."[21] Bardon indirectly presents an existentialist approach here as her sense is clearly captured between the lines. She raises questions that are not easily answered, prompting thoughts that are close to the religious approach characterizing nineteenth-century Realism; a realism that disclaimed the conventional religiosity and chose an alternative explanation, based on the sociological and existential approach.[22] Indeed, Bardon refers to Caravaggio's realism stating that it is possible to define it as an existential situation enslaving man and leaving him without a final answer: "Caravaggio cannot be considered realist or popular because he represents the people, but because he paints them in a frame in which they are enslaved against their will, a frame of life whose purpose is beyond their understanding."[23]

Bardon does not see in Caravaggesque realism a quality that sympathizes with the people. Therefore, she does not discuss the subject as Friedlaender does. On the contrary, in her view, this realism is negatively tinted and close to the existentialist approach by reflecting man's inability to choose his frame of life or to understand what the contents of this frame are. Man lives in it unwillingly, lacking the rational means to decipher the meaning of his existence.

Unlike Bardon, who presents the problem indirectly, Gash states categorically that according to his views, Caravaggio is not one of the modest faithful depicted in his works. Gash bases his opinion on detailed documentation, stating that Caravaggio's approach to religious topics raises doubts as to his religiosity. The artist's interest in existential problems related to religion reveals that the ethos is what he was really interested in. The way of living of the believers appealed to him more than the religious drama. Moreover, in his later religious works there are signs indicating a rise in the pessimistic and tragic feelings that overwhelm him as a consequence of his social deterioration. In Gash's opinion, it is indeed possible to argue and disagree on Caravaggio's religiousness, and to find personal, idiosyncratic characteristics in his religious iconography. Therefore, Gash believes that it would be better to refer to Caravaggio, as Charles Dempsey has, as a Stoic or a Cynic, acknowledging the fact that his deep observation of the figures and their behavior enable him to provide them with new life, treating conventional Christian images in a more complex way.[24]

Consequently, the four criteria: Caravaggesque realism, the reflection of the artist's self, the formal equivalents and Caravaggio's religious approach, stress this book's basic assumption: to present Caravaggio as a modernist. The first criterion, dealing with

Caravaggesque realism, links the artist to modernism, due to his un-conventional approach, relying only on the "existent," on the experi-enced, on the acknowledged. The second criterion, concerning the imprint of the self links Caravaggio to modernism by showing that there is no objective, conclusive truth for all, but only subjective truth. This approach is identified with twentieth-century art concep-tions, stating that there are no conclusive, irrefutable standpoints, but just changing, relative ones. The third criterion, referring to for-mal equivalents, links the artist to modernism by the fact that his paintings do not reflect an outwardly objective reality: the formal el-ement is equivalent to the artist's inner reality. The fourth criterion, concerning the religious approach, reveals that Caravaggio's world is mechanic; it lacks a guiding hand and is denied of any salvation pro-spect, thus being surprisingly close to an existentialist approach.

So far, Caravaggio's work has been referred to relying on the icono-graphic and formal aspects. However, it would be proper to conclude by observing it from a philosophical and aesthetic aspect. To this end, I shall consider Thomas Munro's naturalistic approach already mentioned from his "Meanings of Naturalism in Philosophy and Aesthetics."[25] According to Munro, the naturalistic approach in art history and art criticism reflects only apparent things without at-taching them any transcendental meaning. The "existent" is a unique reference point and, therefore it is a supreme value placed above all other criteria of beauty or nobility.

In metaphysics or general philosophy, the concept of naturalism has a wider meaning. In these fields, naturalism is in opposition to any form of super-naturalism, or transcendentalism, like mysticism, dualism, and idealism. In this domain, naturalism describes phe-nomena by means of proofs based on the sensually perceived, arriv-ing to logical conclusions. This naturalism does not intend a reduc-tion of man's value but an understanding of his real essence. In other words, it relies on the exclusive empiric outlook, without considering the transcendental source towards a comprehension of the world or relying on a-priori evaluations. This is an attempt to understand the nature of man, without adopting any ideological stand ahead, but just understanding it through observation. Therefore, the characteristics of naturalism in aesthetics and general philosophy are materialism, or an approach based on the "existing," the mechanic, and a lack of an intentional, theological explanation. Again and plainly put, it is a purely empiric approach based on the existence in this world.

This approach based solely on the "existing" is connected to the first criterion, which deals with Caravaggesque realism. Non-determination of a-priori theories concerning the individual, and instead, arriving at conclusions based solely on empiric observation, are linked to the second criterion, the reflection of the self, because it is the self which ultimately determinates its own unique reality. Therefore, unusual meanings remain hidden under potentially misleading iconographic guise, essentially opposed to the principles of religion, and based on Caravaggio's self.[26]

A lack of a-priori stands, or religious dogma directing man's behavior, fits the fourth criterion which deals with Caravaggio's religious approach, and brings one to the conclusion that in fact, Caravaggio was not a believer, but, on the contrary, the interpretation of the religious motifs in his work is personal and unique.[27] It seems that if Caravaggio indeed believes in *force majeure* of any kind, this force is not essentially positive. If, nevertheless, one is forced to accept the assumption that Caravaggio is one of the believers he depicts, it may at least be said that his belief is peculiarly expressed, and so arouse the wrath of the Church and its representatives.

Gershom Scholem's book on the main trends of Jewish mysticism might indirectly help to clarify this baffling matter. Scholem sustains that unlike religion, mysticism enables the expression of individual feelings, which is precisely why the orthodoxy is so apprehensive of the mystics, particularly because mysticism sometimes uses orthodox vocabulary to convey thoughts beyond conventional religion.[28] Founded on individual feelings and interpretations, which are naturally opposed to the valid general dogma, mysticism is based on subjectivity, whereas religion is based on objective truths valid for all believers. I certainly do not intend to present Caravaggio as a mystic, but I do sustain that, like a mystic, Caravaggio uses conventional language and iconography in order to convey to the viewer contents that might be interpreted as heresy. Due to the outer "façade" of the work some relate to him as belonging to the conventional frames of religious dogma and some even refer to him as having a strong religious awareness. Nevertheless and above all, Caravaggio is a victim of his desires and nefarious character, as much in the realm of creativity as in real life, precisely because he deviates from conventions and relied on his creative spirit.

The individual, unique characteristics applicable to the whole of his creation enable me to present Caravaggio as a modernist. I shall conclude with a few apt lines from a poem by the symbolist poet, Albert Aurier, from his *L'œuvre maudit* which he justly dedicated to Caravaggio (presented on the following page):

We are the cursed, the
Excommunicated,
Bearing the burden of
Our denied works of art
We have despised the honey
Of purgatories
And vomited toward the sky our
Blasphemous cries
We have said: let us escape
The banal processions
Let us roam the nights alone
Without candles or torches
Let us not follow anymore
The vain river that flows
Let us run with lifted flags
Where the crowds do not go ...

Nous sommes les maudits, les
Excommuniés
Trainant comme un boulet, nos
Chefs d'œuvres niés
Nous avons dédaigné le miel
Des purgatoires
Et vomi vers le ciel nos cris
Blasphématoires
Nous avons dit: Fuyons les
Cortèges banaux
Errons par les nuits seuls,
Sans cierges ni fanaux
Ne soyons plus le fleuve
Vain qui se déroule
Courons drapeaux dressés
Où ne va pas la foule ... [29]

Notes

Introduction

1. For these very reasons, for the remainder of the book the term shall appear with a lowercase "m." Where it appears with a capital it is to denote the chronological/historical period as mentioned above.

2. John Russell, *The Meanings of Modern Art* (New York: Thames and Hudson, 1981), 126, 298.

3. Leopold Zahn, *Kleine Geschichte der modernen Kunst* (Berlin: Verlag das goldene Vlies, 1961), 11–12.

4. Moshe Barasch, *Machshevet ha'omanut badorot ha'acharonim [Approaches to Art 1750–1950]* (Jerusalem: Bialik Institute, 1977), 69–70. Barasch bases himself on: Jacob Burckhardt, *Der Cicerone: eine Anleitung zum Genuss der Kunstwerke Italiens* (Leipzig: EA Seemann, 1879), 407–8.

5. Burckhardt, *Der Cicerone*, 667.

6. Herbert Read, *The Philosophy of Modern Art: Collected Essays* (London: Faber, 1971), 108–9 compares the classical principle to a shell, while the romantic principle he compares to a kernel, because of its vitality, creativity and freedom of expression.

7. Ibid., 110. Read does not refer to the terms "classicism" and "romanticism" as indications of chronological periods but as permanent principles which indicate a particular state of mind and thus he joins the list of above mentioned scholars who consider modernism according to essential values.

CHAPTER 1

1.   Roman Jacobson, "On Realism in Art," in *Language in Literature*, eds. Krystyna Pomorska and Stephen Rudy (Cambridge: Belknap, 1987), 269–73.

2.   Thomas Munro, "Meanings of Naturalism in Philosophy and Aesthetics," *The Journal of Aesthetics and Art Criticism* 19, no. 2 (1960): 133–7.

3.   Linda Nochlin, *Realism: Style and Civilization* (New York: Penguin, 1971), 13–59.

4.   Ibid., 15.

5.   In this context, one has to comprehend the wills of artists as Monet or Constable. One expresses an impossible wish to be born blind and recuperate the sight later; the other, to forget the artistic creations which he ever saw when confronting nature. Both artists express, by means of their requests, an ability of a subjective point of view uninfluenced by what is seen and learnt from the past, based on a kind of utopia anchored exclusively on the values of subjectivity.

6.   Ibid.

7.   Nochlin mentions romantic artists and scholars who deal with Romanticism as this period is based on feelings and a subjective point of view, also when religious conventional iconography is dealt with, as, for example, one can observe in the work of William Blake or Caspar Friedrich.

8.   A significant principle of realism—namely, adhering to the contemporary, seems to necessarily define modernism in the nineteenth century as well. Charles Baudelaire addresses this matter in his essay, "Le peintre de la vie moderne:"

> Alas for the one who approaches ancient art in order to draw from it more than pure art, logic, or a general system. If he delves too deeply into ancient art, one might lose the memory of the present, abandon the rights and values granted by circumstances, for all our originality is the result of the stamp of time on our senses.
>
> (Malheur à celui qui étudie dans l'antique autre chose que l'art pur, la logique, la méthode générale. Pour s'y trop plonger, il perd la mémoire du présent; il abdique la valeur et les privilèges fournis par la circonstance; car presque toute notre originalité vient de l'estampille que le temps imprime à nos sensations.)

See: Charles Baudelaire, "Le peintre de la vie moderne," in *Œuvres complètes: texte établi et annoté*, eds. Yves Gérard Le Dantec and Claude Pichois (Paris: Gallimard, 1976), 696. This and all subsequent translations of any source in French are by the author unless otherwise mentioned.

9. Stéphane Mallarmé, "The Impressionists and Édouard Manet," in *Modern Art and Modernism: A Critical Anthology*, eds. Francis Frascina, Charles Harrison, and Deirdre Paul (New York: Sage, 1982), 39–44.

10. Meyer Schapiro, *Modern Art: Nineteenth and Twentieth Centuries* (New York: G. Braziller, 1982), 50–62.

11. Nochlin, *Realism*, 57–101.

12. Baudelaire, "Le peintre de la vie moderne," 694 expresses a similar idea writing that if the artist wishes to suggest the eternal in the work of art, he should be inspired by the surrounding and the temporary.

13. John Gash, *Caravaggio* (London: Jupiter, 1980), 41.

14. "[I]l Caravaggio disse, che tanta manifattura gli era a fare un quadro di fiori, come di figure." Vincenzo was a member of the Giustiniani family, patrons of Caravaggio. Quoted in: Howard Hibbard, *Caravaggio* (London: Thames and Hudson, 1983), 83.

15. It is unclear whether independent paintings of still-life—and not as part of background to figures—were a significant genre of their own in Italy during Caravaggio's times. Walter Friedlaender claims that the motif of still-life is present before Caravaggio's time and is frequent mainly in France, Spain, and the northern countries. He cites Giovanni Baglione (1566–1643) who praises his friend, the painter Mao Salini (a contemporary of Baglione as well as of Caravaggio's) for his being "the first to paint flowers in vases."

It is also credulous whether Caravaggio himself painted still-life pictures during his youth. Friedlaender deduces from the above quote that Caravaggio indeed created still-life pictures. It is clear, though, as I am proposing, that Caravaggio is aware of various iconographic and formal traditions in painting and utilizes them in a distinctly novel way. On the debates on still-life in Italy and in Caravaggio and Baglione's quote, see: Walter Friedlaender, *Caravaggio Studies* (Princeton: Princeton University Press, 1973), 80, 143 respectively. On Baglione, see also notes 40 and 42 below.

16. James Hall, *Dictionary of Subjects and Symbols in Art* (New York: Harper and Row, 1974), 291, 330–1. Observing the art of the north, one learns that these fruits are linked to the motif of the Resurrection of Jesus, frequently appearing in this context, as, for example, in the painting by Joos van Cleve *The Holy Family* (fig. 2).

17. Ibid., 291.

18. See, for comparison, the traditional iconography of the fruits in Caravaggio's *Supper at Emmaus* (fig. 3) and the connotation of sexuality of *vanitas* and of Prudence in his *Boy Bitten by a Lizard* (fig. 4) as discussed in: Hibbard, *Caravaggio*, 44–5, 75.

19. Erwin Panofsky, *Early Netherlandish Painting: Its Origins and Character* (New York: Harper and Row, 1971), 131–2.

20. Kenneth Clark, *Landscape into Art* (New York: Penguin, 1984), 33–71.

21. A comparison between the symbolism pertaining to the religious convention and the Symbolism as a style of the nineteenth and twentieth centuries, anchored solely on personal symbolism, should be of interest.

22. Johan Huizinga, *The Waning of the Middle Ages: A Study of the Forms of Life, Thought, and Art in France and the Netherlands in the Fourteenth and Fifteenth Centuries* (New York: Bucks, 1976), 136. Emphasis in the original.

23. In the book by Gershom Scholem, which will be mentioned later, the author writes a general introduction on the subject of mysticism as a phenomenon and mentions the danger deriving from the usage of conventional iconography by mystics, as they grant meanings contradicting the spirit of tradition. For Scholem's book, see Summary, pp. 70–1, n. 28.

24. Friedlaender states that Caravaggio may, therefore, be compared to Manet and Cézanne: "For its time, such a dictum was almost 'subversive,' anticipating the scale of values of Manet and Cézanne." See: Friedlaender, *Caravaggio Studies*, 143.

25. "His achievement was based on looking inward, on imagination coupled with a special sense of humanity in the service of traditional religious scenes. Caravaggio's novelty was poetic, for all his 'realism.'" See: Hibbard, *Caravaggio*, 85.

26. André Chastel and Angela Ottino Della Chiesa, *Tout l'œuvre peinte du Caravage* (Paris: Éditions de Minuit, 1959), 21.

27. Nochlin, *Realism*, 236.

28. The legitimacy to see reality in a personal way without being subdued to dogmas which do not pertain to the domain of the arts introduces subjectivity. The legitimacy to observe external reality as it appears to the individual eye, physically and spiritually, bears the seeds of the abstract trend in the arts. One may consider abstract art as an externalization of a state of mind. It is of no surprise, therefore, that Monet and Cézanne reached the threshold of abstract art.

29. Michael Kitson, *The Complete Paintings of Caravaggio* (London: Weidenfeld and Nicolson, 1969), 9.

30. Friedlaender, *Caravaggio Studies*, 82–3; Hibbard, *Caravaggio*, 24. Additional examples for paintings of this sort given by Friedlaender are: Quentin Massys's *Ill-Matched Lovers* (c. 1520/5), Jan Sanders van Hemessen's *Loose Company* (1543) and Marinus van Reymerswaele's *The Money Changer and His Wife* (1539).

31. Giovanni Pietro Bellori was a painter and an archeological and art critic. His book on the lives of artists of his time is thought to be of equal importance as that of Vassari's a century earlier. On Bellori, see: Hibbard, *Caravaggio*, 360.

32. Ibid., 47, 362.

33. Ibid., 371–2. Notwithstanding, Bellori claims that Caravaggio's work is too radical, as his descriptions tend to an extreme realism, to an imitation of negative elements, and to a search of the dirty and the distorted.

34. Hibbard, *Caravaggio*, 24.

35. The following (and additional) information on Mary and its origin in primary sources can be found in: Émile Mâle, *L'art religieux du XIIᵉ siècle en France: étude sur l'iconographie de moyen âge et sur ses sources d'inspiration* (Paris: Librairie Armand Collin, 1958), 2:174–96.

36. Hibbard, *Caravaggio*, 204.

37. A painting by Quentin Massys depicting the death of St. Anne (fig. 8), follows similar iconographic formulae. Her head is covered and she is holding the candle of faith amid the mourners, but there is no concretization of the mystic light characterizing Jesus and no heavenly entourage.

38. Giulio Mancini was an amateur collector who also became Pope Urban VIII's private doctor in the 1620s. His writings, concerning Italian painters and a catalogue of art in churches during his time, are of the first and basic sources for information about Caravaggio. On Mancini, see: Ibid., 7, n. 12.

39. See Mancini's *Considerazioni sulla pittura* in: Ibid., 346.

40. Giovanni Baglione was a painter, contemporary of Caravaggio's and his adversary. He offered a short account of Caravaggio's career in Rome in his book on artistic activity between 1572 and 1642. On Baglione, see: Ibid., 7, 351.

41. Gash ponders whether the Carmelites who used to walk barefoot rejected the work because Mary was depicted barefoot. He suggests that the real reason was her undue description as Counter-Reformation wished to stress Mary's death as passage and not ultimate death. See: Gash, *Caravaggio*, 104.

42. See Giovanni Baglione's *Le vite de' pittori, scultori, architetti ...* from 1642 in: Hibbard, *Caravaggio*, 351–5.

CHAPTER 2

1. Charles Baudelaire, "L'art philosophique," in *Œuvres complètes*, 598.

2. Baudelaire, "Salon de 1859," in Ibid., 655.

3. Robert Rosenblum, *Cubism and Twentieth-Century Art* (New York: HN Abrams, 1976), 65–6.

4. Rosenblum, *Modern Painting and the Northern Romantic Tradition: Friedrich to Rothko* (London: Thames and Hudson, 1975), 45–6.

5. Ibid., 62.

6. See, for example, motifs of children and flowers in the work of Otto Runge which can be comprehended empirically indicating the microcosms and the finality of things, as well as symbols of the divine creation and the macrocosms. See also motifs of ships and trees in the work of Caspar Friedrich.

7. Phoebe Pool, *Impressionism* (London: Thames and Hudson, 1981), 9.

8. Hugh Honour, *Romanticism* (New York: Allen Lane, 1979), 14–18.

9. Read, *The Philosophy of Modern Art*, 93–4.

10. Naum Gabo, "A Retrospective View of Constructive Art," in *Three Lectures on Modern Art: "Intrinsic Significance" in Modern Art*, ed. Katherine Sophie Dreier (New York: Philosophical Library, 1949).

11. Read, *The Philosophy of Modern Art*, 116–7 shows the link between Romanticism and Surrealism, as Pool has done between Romanticism and Impressionism. Read also writes about the difference existing between the internal subjective world and the objective external world, a schism which does not bring with it tranquility or spiritual stability, therefore the solution has to be carried out by a synthesis including both the subjective element and the objective element. This synthesis serves as an experience of a different kind.

12. Germain Bazin, *Baroque and Rococo Art*, trans. Jonathan Griffin (London: Thames and Hudson, 1979), 43.

13. Kitson, *The Complete Paintings of Caravaggio*, 7. On this subject there is documentation according to which the artist had to leave Syracuse (Sicily) after quarreling with the school principal who did not approve of the special attention Caravaggio showed to young male pupils. See the remark by Susini in: Friedlaender, *Caravaggio Studies*, 133.

14. Longhi in his *Vita Artistica* from 1927, mentioned in: Ibid., 146.

15. On Mancini and Alciati's *Emblemata*, see: Gash, *Caravaggio*, 32 and Hibbard, *Caravaggio*, 21.

16. Hall, *Dictionary*, 264.

17. Kenneth Clark, *The Nude: A Study in Ideal Art* (Princeton: Princeton University Press, 1956), 264.

18. The other three categories are the energetic, the pathetic, and the sinner. The energetic is where the body is controlled by the power of will; the pathetic is where the body is defeated by pain, obstacles or fate. The pathetic man suffers because of the gods' wrath. The defeat of the body by the spirit might be interpreted as the gods' triumph over matter; the sinner type of nude is different from the others in form. The beauty factor has been changed by a feeling of shame and an

awareness of sin. The nude gets an inferior, satanic dimension, a kind of embodiment of spirit in matter whose values are different. See: Ibid., 214, 265–6, 301.

19. This is probably the reason why the work was catalogued as "*satiro*" (satyr) in the inventory of the Borghese collection compiled in 1760. On the missing vines and glass, see: Friedlaender, *Caravaggio Studies*, 146.

20. In this sense this Bacchus conforms to the type of the pathetic body advanced by Clark. See notes 17–18 above.

21. Chastel and Della Chiesa, *Tout l'œuvre*, 8.

22. "To the Romantic artist—by nature essentially and intimately a passionate individualist, a spontaneous creator—any norm was deeply antipathetic." Honour, *Romanticism*, 14. See chapter 2, p. 21, n. 8.

23. "[h]e who says Romanticism, says Modern Art." Baudelaire, "Salon de 1846," in *Œuvres complètes*, 420–1.

24. Ovide, *Les Métamorphoses*, trans. Joseph Chamonard (Paris: Garnier-Flammarion, 1966), 129, 132, 141.

25. Friedlaender, *Caravaggio Studies*, 87.

26. Michael Avi Yonah, *Toldot ha'omanut haklasit [A History of Classical Art]* (Jerusalem: Bialik Institute, 1969), 36.

27. See: Friedlaender, *Caravaggio Studies*, 88, n. 4.

28. It is possible that the image of the Medusa is, yet again, but a self-portrait of the artist, for which purpose he would use a mirror. Thus, Caravaggio followed Perseus who was able to overcome the monster only by using a mirror. See: Ibid., 87.

29. Linda Murray, *Michelangelo* (London: Thames and Hudson, 1980), 41–2.

30. Murray even goes as far as to claim to see the aspects of the sermons delivered by the Dominican friar Girolamo Savonarola (1452–1498) manifested in the statue. Savonarola fought against the roots of evil, which, in his view, were caused by materialism. He was an extremist who had a hysterical influence over the city of Florence, especially in 1494. In 1497, he was arrested by the governors, following demonstrations caused by a trial. The accused in that specific trail was one of Savonarola's followers, who had threatened to burn himself alive in order to prove his master's sanctity. Savonarola himself was suspected of heresy and, together with two of his supporters, was tortured, crucified and burnt. See: Ibid., 40–2.

31. Friedlaender, *Caravaggio Studies*, 202–3. For Bellori's text mentioned by Friedlender (p. 214 in it), see: Hibbard, *Caravaggio*, 373.

32. On this painting, see chapter 3, p. 35.

33. See documents on Caravaggio's life in: Friedlaender, *Caravaggio Studies*, 267–93. This painting was made one or two years before his death. It might serve

as a summing-up of his life. In 1605, Caravaggio assaulted a notary, one Mariano Pasqualoni of Accumoli, over a well-known courtesan and model of his by the name of Lena. Aware of his dark sides, but unable to avoid them, he expressed after the outburst:

> I, Michelangelo Merisi, having been insulted by Mr. Maryno, clerk of the Vicar's Court, as he would not wear a sword in the daytime, resolved to strike him wherever I should meet him. One night, having come upon him accompanied by another man and having perfectly recognized his face, I struck him. I am very sorry for what I did, and if I had not done it yet, I would not do it. I beg him for his forgiveness and peace, and regard the said Mr. Maryno with a sword in his hand as a man fit to stand his ground against me or anybody else.
> I, Michelangelo Merisi, do affirm all the above.

According to this statement, Caravaggio the aggressor asks for pardon. He affirms though, that the victim, as any other man, is his equal when armed. Paradoxically, the victim was unarmed when attacked. See: Ibid., 284–6.

CHAPTER 3

1. Paul Sérusier and Maurice Denis, *ABC de la peinture: suivi d'une étude sur la vie et l'œuvre de Paul Sérusier par Maurice Denis* (Paris: Floury, 1942), 105.

2. Herbert Read, *A Concise History of Modern Sculpture* (London: Thames and Hudson, 1964), 11.

3. Harold Rosenberg, *The Tradition of the New* (Chicago: University of Chicago Press, 1982), 18.

4. On Picasso and Gris in the following, see: Read, *Philosophy of Modern Art*, 91–3.

5. Gris uses a metaphor of a cloth made by two series of threads. The one represents the figurative aspect, and the other, the abstract. The threads intercross, inter-depend, and complement each other. When one series of threads is absent, the cloth ceases to exist. Gris fulfills the formal equivalents in a complex way: he starts with the mathematical idea and ends with the world of appearances. See: Ibid., 92.

6. Ibid., 98–9.

7. Rosenblum, *Cubism and Twentieth-Century Art*, 14.

8. "La rechercher des schémas formels abstraits est une nécessité, chez Caravage, à ce moment-là, précisément parce qu'il refuse l'apriorisme littéraire pour sa peinture, parce qu'il a besoin, pour créer une nouvelle connaissance du réel par la

peinture, de passer par l'abstraction, parce qu'il lui faut inventer une iconographie ou la signification ne soit pas séparée de la forme." See : Françoise Bardon, *Caravage ou, L'Expérience de la matière* (Paris: Presses universitaires de France, 1978), 57.

9. "En fait, il [Caravage] est le peintre le plus abstrait de son temps et le plus *réaliste parce qu'abstrait*. Il réussit à montrer la réalité de son temps parce qu'il l'objective. Son 'réalisme' est un réalisme de la connaissance et non de la vision immédiate." See: Ibid., 124. Emphasis in the original.

10. Bardon does not elaborate on this matter, though. Picasso's words on his own art will assist, however, in understanding the idea according to which the abstract element does help to comprehend reality, and is an integral part of it. According to Picasso, quoted in Mario de Michelli's *Sciritti de Picasso*:

> Abstract art never gets beyond painting. So, what's the excitement? There is no such thing as abstract art. You have to start from somewhere. You can completely remove any appearance of reality but the idea of the object will somehow have left its ineradicable sign: because it is the object that has touched the artist, that has excited his ideas, that has stirred his emotions. In the final analysis, ideas and emotions are rooted in his work. They are an integral part of it even if their presence is not evident. Whether he likes it or not, man is an instrument of nature, which imposes its character and its appearance on him.

Picasso then elaborates: "Moreover, there is no such thing as figurative or nonfigurative art. Everything appears to us in the form of a figure. Even in metaphysics ideas are expressed through figures, so obviously it would be absurd to think of a painting without figuration."

In a letter to Florent Fels, quoted in *Bulletin de la Vie Artistique*, he writes: "[…W]e speak of naturalism as opposed to modern art. But have you ever seen a 'natural' work of art? As nature and art are two perfectly different phenomena, they cannot be subordinated to the same subject. Art gives us the possibility of expressing our conception and our understanding of what nature cannot give us in absolute form." Both quotes are in: Domenico Porzio and Marco Valsecchi, *Pablo Picasso: Man and His Work* (New York: Chartwell, 1973), 81 and 85 respectively.

11. In the chapter dealing with the reflection of the self in Caravaggio's work, I have dealt at length with the subject of David and Goliath. The two represent two aspects of the artist's personality—the murdered and the murderer—as a sort of severe mental state in which the artist is aware of his obscure nature, but nevertheless cannot overcome his horrid instinct. See chapter 2, pp. 28–30.

12. Hibbard, *Caravaggio*, 66.

13. Bardon, *Caravage*, 64–5.

14. Chastel and Della Chiesa, *Tout l'œuvre*, 1.

15. Bardon, *Caravage*, 70.

16. Ibid., 67–8.

17. Ibid., 34–48.

18. Friedlaender, *Caravaggio Studies*, 3–28.

19. On the first version of *The Conversion of St. Paul*, see: Hibbard, *Caravaggio*, 121–5.

20. Ibid., 123.

21. "[…] non pas l'événement, mais son résultat, le *hic et nunc* de la chose." [not the event itself, but its result, the here and now of the matter.] Bardon, *Caravage*, 108.

22. Friedlaender suggests that Dürer might have been Caravaggio's source of inspiration in the depiction of a labor animal. See: Friedlaender, *Caravaggio Studies*, 8–9.

23. Ibid., 10.

24. Friedlaender leaves these "scientists and rationalists" wittingly anonymous. See: Ibid., 24.

25. Horst Woldemar Janson, *History of Art* (London: Thames and Hudson, 1976), 484. Janson also mentions the great influence that Caravaggio's creation had on Rembrandt. On same state of mind, see: Hibbard, *Caravaggio*, 128, 131.

26. Arnold Hauser, *Historia social de la literatura y el arte* (Madrid: Guadarrama, 1969), 110–11.

27. Ernst Hans Gombrich, *L'art et son histoire des origines à nos jours* (Paris: R. Julliard, 1963), 93–4.

28. Chastel and Della Chiesa, *Tout l'œuvre*, 1–3.

29. Bardon, *Caravage*, 108–11.

30. Bernard Berenson, *Caravaggio: His Incongruity and His Fame* (London: Chapman and Hall, 1953), 19–20.

31. Peter Fuller, *Art and Psychoanalysis* (London: Writers and Readers, 1980), 43–4.

32. Leonardo da Vinci and Michelangelo adopt Alberti's view. For them, *expresia* was linked to a careful study of human anatomy. Indeed, many of the Renaissance artists learned anatomy and dissected bodies.

33. Bardon, *Caravage*, 57. See p. 41, n. 17.

34. Gash, *Caravaggio*, 7.

CHAPTER 4

1. See the notion of religion as understood by Romantic artists as Caspar Friedrich, Otto Runge and William Blake, whose belief is stamped by personal symbolism in opposition to the iconography pertaining to the collective dogma in: Honour, *Romanticism*, 24–7, 72. See also the vicious sides of the divinity in: Kathleen Raine, *William Blake* (Oxford: Oxford University Press, 1970), 76–94 and Geoffrey Keynes, *Drawings of William Blake* (Mineola, NY: Dover, 1970), 21–3.

2. Nochlin, *Realism*, 57–101.

3. Hall, *Dictionary*, 205. On painters that influenced Caravaggio on the presentation of this subject, see: Hibbard, *Caravaggio*, 138–43.

4. Hibbard, *Caravaggio*, 365.

5. Ibid., 353.

6. Bardon, *Caravage*, 132.

7. In *The Cardsharps*, as I have shown, one does not know on whose side the artist is; the same is true for *David with the Head of Goliath* and *Medusa*, where the artist does not morally distinguishes between victim and offender. The same ambivalence holds for *Death of the Virgin*, where the human side overpowers the divine, opposing traditional thinking. See chapter 2.

8. Kitson, *The Complete Paintings of Caravaggio*, 6.

9. Chastel and Della Chiesa, *Tout l'œuvre*, 8.

10. Bardon cites as source *La Légende Dorée*. See: Bardon, *Caravage*, 77; Friedlaender cites the *Acta Sanctorum*. See: Friedlaender, *Caravaggio Studies*, 179.

11. See chapter 3, pp. 42–5.

12. Gash, *Caravaggio*, 94 bases his opinion on a painting *c.* 1621 by Ottavio Leoni (1578–1630) supposed to be Caravaggio's portrait.

13. Friedlaender, *Caravaggio Studies*, 180.

14. Hall, *Dictionary*, 231–2.

15. On the traditional depiction of St. Matthew, see: Friedlaender, *Caravaggio Studies*, 110–6.

16. Mâle, *L'art religieux*, 37.

17. See note 11 above.

18. Such a particular composition also takes place in *The Martyrdom of St. Matthew*, where the cross is made up by the saint's body itself. See chapter 4, p. 55.

19. Bardon, *Caravage*, 102–3.

20. Hibbard, *Caravaggio*, 134.

21. On this painting and Ribera, see: Valeriano Bozal, *Historia del Arte en España* (Madrid: Istmo, 1972), 180–4.

22. Bardon, *Caravage*, 103–4 describes this darkness as "nocturnal matter" (matière nocturne), stressing two facts: one, the subject at hand is material; two, this material is made of the night.

23. Friedlaender, *Caravaggio Studies*, 151–2 detects the influence of Giorgione in Caravaggio's depiction of landscapes.

24. Linda Murray, *The High Renaissance and Mannerism* (London: Thames and Hudson, 1977), 201.

25. Compare also Caravaggio's withdrawn Mary—inwards both mentally and spatially in the painting—to another un-haloed but frontal, rosy-cheeked, lively Mary of Joos van Cleve's *Holy Family* mentioned earlier. See note 16 to chapter 1.

26. Hall, *Dictionary*, 334.

27. Gash, *Caravaggio*, 90.

28. Friedlaender, *Caravaggio Studies*, 190.

29. Bardon, *Caravage*, 135.

30. Kitson, *The Complete Paintings of Caravaggio*, 9.

Summary

1. "… [A]rt is nothing but a bagatelle or children's work, whatever it is and whoever it is by, unless it is done after life […] for to paint after a drawing, however close it may be to life, is not as good as following Nature with all her various colors." Carel van Mander was the first Netherlandish theoretician of art and he stayed in Italy between 1573 and 1577. He surveyed Italian artists while staying there and mentions Caravaggio as well in his copious series *Schilder-boeck*. He is quoted in: Hibbard, *Caravaggio*, 343–4.

2. Ibid., vii.

3. Ibid., 344.

4. Janson, *History of Art*, 483–4.

5. Kitson, *The Complete Paintings of Caravaggio*, 5.

6. Ibid., 6.

7. Francesco Scannelli, like Mancini mentioned earlier, was a doctor and a dilettante in painting. He wrote a book on Italian painting as manifested in four major schools he detected. Extract from his *Il microcosm della pittura …* on Caravaggio and short biographical information are in: Hibbard, *Caravaggio*, 356–60.

8. "[… H]e lacked the necessary basis for good design, producing faulty creations without completely achieving a beautiful conception, gracefulness, decorum, architecture, perspective, or other similar and significant elements that together render sufficiently worthy the true principles of the great masters." See: Ibid., 357.

9. Ibid., vii.

10. Gash, *Caravaggio*, 20–1.

11. Sérusier and Denis, *ABC de la peinture*, 105.

12. See the ideas of Albert Aurier according to which there are correspondences between the spiritual world and the natural world; things existing in the natural world through the spiritual one are called "representations." See: Philippe Jullian, *The Symbolists* (New York: Phaidon, 1973), 15.

13. Gash, *Caravaggio*, 20.

14. Frank Stella is a contemporary artist related to Post-Painterly Abstraction. He links himself directly with Caravaggio. After visiting Rome, he felt it was worth to be a painter, if only to do what Caravaggio and Rubens did before him. He does not sense any distance between him and Caravaggio, because three or four centuries are meaningless when one stands in front of a work of art. Like Caravaggio, Stella grants and translates his feelings and moods to formal equivalents, thus feeling as a follower of Caravaggio, disregarding the time gap.

Stella's thoughts on Caravaggio are expressed in a *New Yorker* profile article by Calvin Tomkins. The views brought here are presented there and in Stella's own comments on Caravaggio. On Stella specifically, see: Edward Lucie-Smith, *Art Today: From Abstract Expressionism to Surrealism* (New York: Phaidon, 1981), 340–7. For the profile article, see: Calvin Tomkins, "The Space Around Real Things," *The New Yorker*, 10 September 1984. For Stella's text, see: Frank Stella, *Working Space* (Harvard: Harvard University Press, 1986), 1–22.

15. These sentiments are expressed by Bardon as well. See chapter 3, pp. 34–5.

16. In his article Tomkins does not refer to Stella's ideas either systematically or logically. However, it could be concluded that Stella sees the link between Caravaggio's realism and nineteenth-century Realism because of the legitimacy to consider the object as an object, with no further meaning. Realism opens the gates towards a natural development ending in Impressionism, so that an artist like Monet, for instance, reaches the threshold of abstraction, while an artist like Van Gogh reaches Expressionism. In other words, an independent outlook regarding external appearances, as well as the legitimacy to externalize internal feelings, are the forebears of the abstract in Modernism. (On this subject, see also: Nochlin, *Realism*, 144.)

In the *New Yorker* article Stella explains that Cubism is not necessarily the beginning of abstraction, for there is still much to inquire about abstraction and its primordial characteristic—to free art from all illustrative remains. Caravaggio sets the foundations of art's future development. Therefore, Stella does not recoil from mentioning the names of Caravaggio and Rubens together with Wassily Kandinski, Kasimir Malevich and Piet Mondrian, due to the dramatic power and the emphasis on the pictorial foundations of their works. The astounding innovations of these artists contribute to the breakthrough of Abstract Expressionism at the end of the 1950s, and to artists, like Jackson Pollock, Willem De Kooning, Franz Klein, Arshile Gorki, Mark Rothko, Barnett Newman and Clifford Still. Stella believes that these artists produced an outburst of pictorial energy whose strength is comparable to that of Rubens' in the seventeenth century. See: Stella, *Working Space*, 21–2.

17. On *St. John the Baptist*, see: Ibid., 10–12.

18. Friedlaender, *Caravaggio Studies*, 23–4.

19. Ibid., 122–35.

20. "the great wheel of human fatalism turns in a void." Bardon, *Caravage*, 139.

21. [l]'angle de la pierre et le noir de la terre qu'elle découpe, sont placés au niveau des yeux du spectateur, de telle sorte que ce dernier reçoive, comme le porteur, tout le poids de la descente et du monde qui se défait, se déplie dans la suite de la mort du Christ, pour laquelle il n'y a pas de résurrection possible. Ibid., 139–40.

22. Ibid., 103.

23. "Caravage n'est ni réaliste ni populaire parce qu'il représente des gens du peuple, mais il est réaliste parce qu'il les peint dans un rapport qui est le leur, rapport ici de subordination à une tache dont la fin les dépasse [...]" Ibid.

24. On Caravaggio's approach to religion and existentialism as presented in this paragraph, see: Gash, *Caravaggio*, 10–11. In order to prove that Caravaggio was actually a heretic, Gash bases himself on an anecdote found in a book by Francesco Susinno (*c.* 1660/70–1739), *The Lives of the Messina Painters*. Sussino (whose name is spelled by earlier writers as "Susino") was a priest who had studied painting in Naples. His *Le vite de' pittori messinesi* of 1724 includes traditional knowledge on Caravaggio and his friend, Mario Minnitti of Syracuse. The anecdote, Gash believes, is in accordance with the spirit of the artist. It tells that when Caravaggio entered the church of the Madonna del Pilero, "[a] most polite [... gentleman] came forward to offer him the holy water, and Caravaggio asked him what it was for; to cancel out venial sins he was told: 'I don't need it', was the reply, 'because mine are all mortal.'" See a longer version of this text in: Hibbard, *Caravaggio*, 380–7.

25. See chapter 1, p. 8, n. 2.

26. This is expressed in *The Beheading of St. John* (fig. 44). Apparently and outwardly, the painting depicts the beheading of St. John according to traditional iconography. However, a deeper look reveals that the saint is none other than

Caravaggio himself. This is concluded from the signature, which has been painted with the blood oozing from the throat, thereby extinguishing his life (See: Ibid., 231). Similarly, and as mentioned before (see chapter 2, pp. 28–30), Caravaggio feels martyred and murdered in *David with the Head of Goliath* (fig. 15) where he appears as both killer and victim. The simultaneous depiction of himself as killer and victim fits the feeling of impotence pervading his works.

27. This interpretation caused some scholars to conclude on his heresy and laity.

28. Gershom Scholem, *Major Trends in Jewish Mysticism* (Jerusalem: Schocken, 1941), 1–10. See also note 23 to chapter 1.

29. Free translation by the author. See original in: Sven Lövgren, *The Genesis of Modernism: Seurat, Gauguin, Van Gogh. French Symbolism in the 1880s* (Bloomington: Indiana University Press, 1971), 138.

BIBLIOGRAPHY

Avi Yonah, Michael. *Toldot ha'omanut haklasit [A History of Classical Art]*. Jerusalem: Bialik Institute, 1969.

Barasch, Moshe. *Machshevet ha'omanut badorot ha'acharonim [Approaches to Art 1750–1950]*. Jerusalem: Bialik Institute, 1977.

Bardon, Françoise. *Caravage ou, L'Expérience de la matière*. Paris: Presses universitaires de France, 1978.

Baudelaire, Charles. "L'art philosophique." In *Œuvres complètes: texte établi et annoté*, edited by Yves Gérard Le Dantec and Claude Pichois. Paris: Gallimard, 1976.

———. "Le peintre de la vie moderne." In *Œuvres complètes: texte établi et annoté*, edited by Yves Gérard Le Dantec and Claude Pichois. Paris: Gallimard, 1976.

———. "Salon de 1846." In *Œuvres complètes: texte établi et annoté*, edited by Yves Gérard Le Dantec and Claude Pichois. Paris: Gallimard, 1976.

———. "Salon de 1859." In *Œuvres complètes: texte établi et annoté*, edited by Yves Gérard Le Dantec and Claude Pichois. Paris: Gallimard, 1976.

Bazin, Germain. *Baroque and Rococo Art*. Translated by Jonathan Griffin. London: Thames and Hudson, 1979.

Bozal, Valeriano. *Historia del Arte en España*. Madrid: Istmo, 1972.

Burckhardt, Jacob. *Der Cicerone: eine Anleitung zum Genuss der Kunstwerke Italiens*. Leipzig: EA Seemann, 1879.

Chastel, André, and Angela Ottino Della Chiesa. *Tout l'œuvre peinte du Caravage*. Paris: Éditions de Minuit, 1959.

Clark, Kenneth. *Landscape into Art*. New York: Penguin, 1984.

———. *The Nude: A Study in Ideal Art*. Princeton: Princeton University Press, 1956.

Friedlaender, Walter. *Caravaggio Studies*. Princeton: Princeton University Press, 1973.

Fuller, Peter. *Art and Psychoanalysis*. London: Writers and Readers, 1980.

Gabo, Naum. "A Retrospective View of Constructive Art." In *Three Lectures on Modern Art: "Intrinsic Significance" in Modern Art*, edited by Katherine Sophie Dreier. New York: Philosophical Library, 1949.

Gash, John. *Caravaggio*. London: Jupiter, 1980.

Gombrich, Ernst Hans. *L'art et son histoire des origines à nos jours*. Paris: R. Julliard, 1963.

Hall, James. *Dictionary of Subjects and Symbols in Art*. New York: Harper and Row, 1974.

Hauser, Arnold. *Historia social de la literatura y el arte*. Madrid: Guadarrama, 1969.

Hibbard, Howard. *Caravaggio*. London: Thames and Hudson, 1983.

Honour, Hugh. *Romanticism*. New York: Allen Lane, 1979.

Huizinga, Johan. *The Waning of the Middle Ages: A Study of the Forms of Life, Thought, and Art in France and the Netherlands in the Fourteenth and Fifteenth Centuries*. New York: Bucks, 1976.

Jacobson, Roman. "On Realism in Art." In *Language in Literature*, edited by Krystyna Pomorska and Stephen Rudy, 19–27. Cambridge: Belknap, 1987.

Janson, Horst Woldemar. *History of Art*. London: Thames and Hudson, 1976.

Jullian, Philippe. *The Symbolists*. New York: Phaidon, 1973.

Keynes, Geoffrey. *Drawings of William Blake*. Mineola, NY: Dover, 1970.

Kitson, Michael. *The Complete Paintings of Caravaggio*. London: Weidenfeld and Nicolson, 1969.

Lövgren, Sven. *The Genesis of Modernism: Seurat, Gauguin, Van Gogh. French Symbolism in the 1880s.* Bloomington: Indiana University Press, 1971.

Lucie-Smith, Edward. *Art Today: From Abstract Expressionism to Surrealism.* New York: Phaidon, 1981.

Mâle, Émile. *L'art religieux du XIIe siècle en France: étude sur l'iconographie du moyen âge et sur ses sources d'inspiration.* Vol. 2. Paris: Librairie Armand Collin, 1958.

Mallarmé, Stéphane. "The Impressionists and Édouard Manet." In *Modern Art and Modernism: A Critical Anthology*, edited by Francis Frascina, Charles Harrison, and Deirdre Paul. New York: Sage, 1982.

Munro, Thomas. "Meanings of Naturalism in Philosophy and Aesthetics." *The Journal of Aesthetics and Art Criticism* 19, no. 2 (1960): 133–37.

Murray, Linda. *Michelangelo.* London: Thames and Hudson, 1980.

———. *The High Renaissance and Mannerism.* London: Thames and Hudson, 1977.

Nochlin, Linda. *Realism: Style and Civilization.* New York: Penguin, 1971.

Ovide. *Les Métamorphoses.* Translated by Joseph Chamonard. Paris: Garnier-Flammarion, 1966.

Panofsky, Erwin. *Early Netherlandish Painting: Its Origins and Character.* New York: Harper and Row, 1971.

Pool, Phoebe. *Impressionism.* London: Thames and Hudson, 1981.

Porzio, Domenico, and Marco Valsecchi. *Pablo Picasso: Man and His Work.* New York: Chartwell, 1973.

Raine, Kathleen. *William Blake.* Oxford: Oxford University Press, 1970.

Read, Herbert. *A Concise History of Modern Sculpture.* London: Thames and Hudson, 1964.

———. *The Philosophy of Modern Art: Collected Essays.* London: Faber, 1971.

Rosenberg, Harold. *The Tradition of the New.* Chicago: University of Chicago Press, 1982.

Rosenblum, Robert. *Cubism and Twentieth-Century Art.* New York: HN Abrams, 1976.

———. *Modern Painting and the Northern Romantic Tradition: Friedrich to Rothko*. London: Thames and Hudson, 1975.

Russell, John. *The Meanings of Modern Art*. New York: Thames and Hudson, 1981.

Schapiro, Meyer. *Modern Art: Nineteenth and Twentieth Centuries*. New York: G. Braziller, 1982.

Scholem, Gershom. *Major Trends in Jewish Mysticism*. Jerusalem: Schocken, 1941.

Sérusier, Paul, and Maurice Denis. *ABC de la peinture: suivi d'une étude sur la vie et l'œuvre de Paul Sérusier par Maurice Denis*. Paris: Floury, 1942.

Stella, Frank. *Working Space*. Harvard: Harvard University Press, 1986.

Tomkins, Calvin. "The Space Around Real Things." *The New Yorker*, September 10, 1984.

Zahn, Leopold. *Kleine Geschichte der modernen Kunst*. Berlin: Verlag das goldene Vlies, 1961.

INDEX

ILLUSTRATIONS

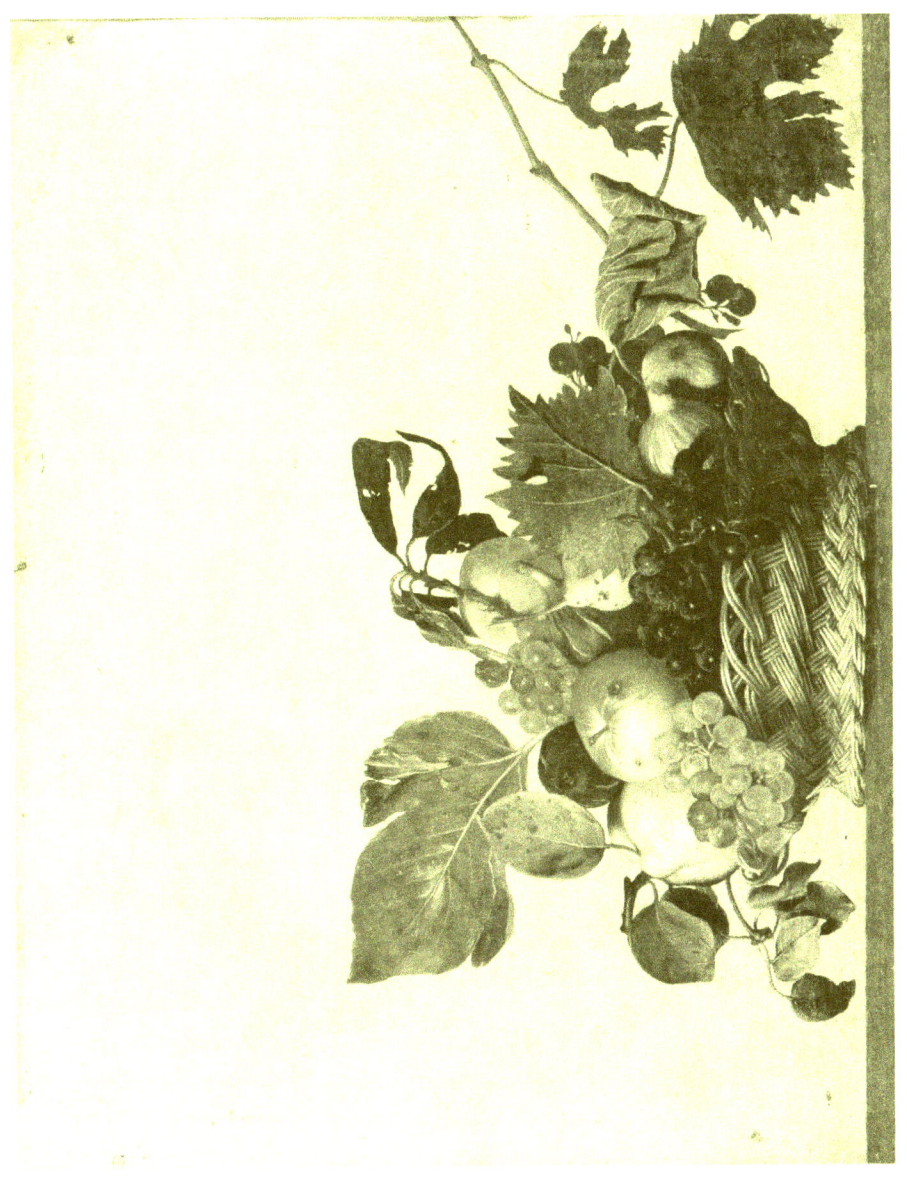

FIGURE NO. 1 ✢ Caravaggio, *Basket of Fruit*, c. 1596

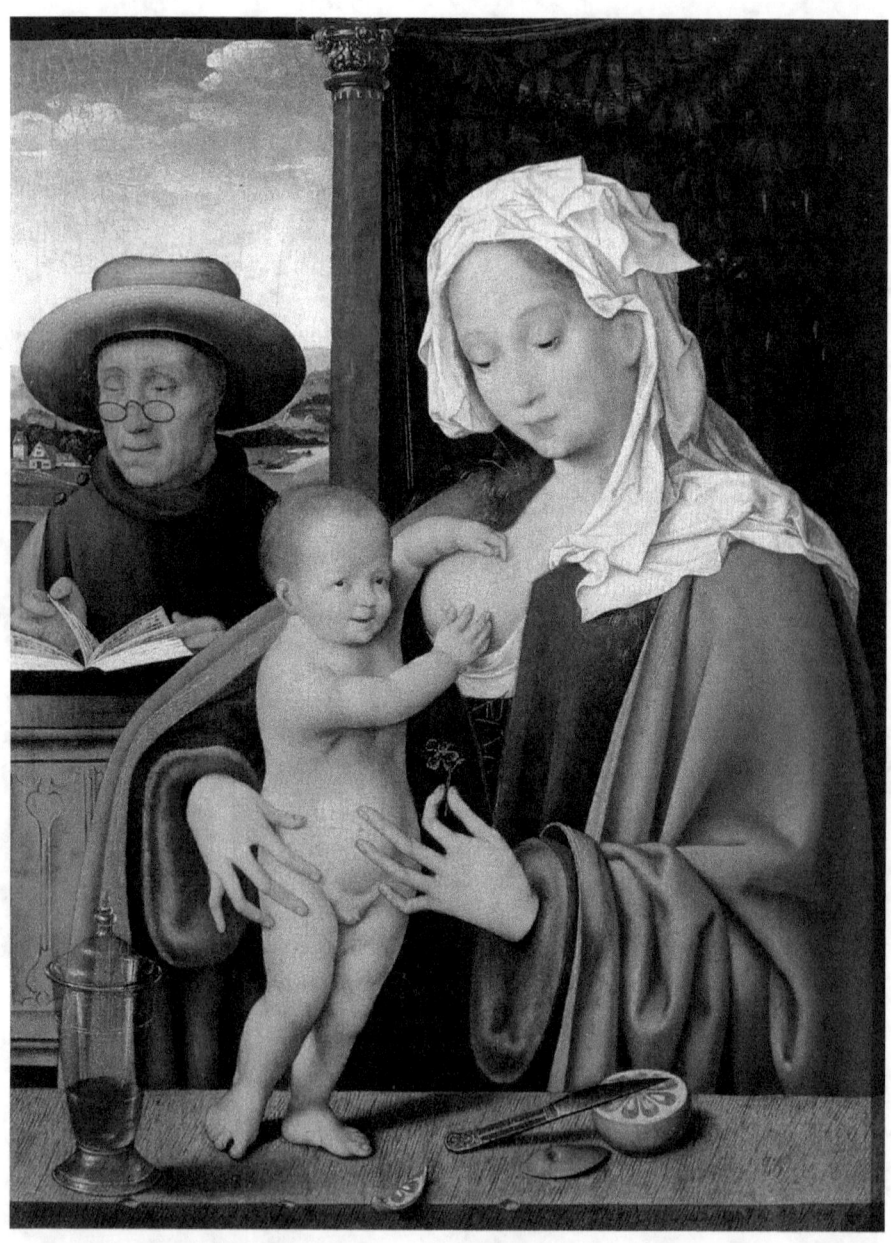

FIGURE NO. 2 ✣ Joos van Cleve, *The Holy Family*, c. 1515–20

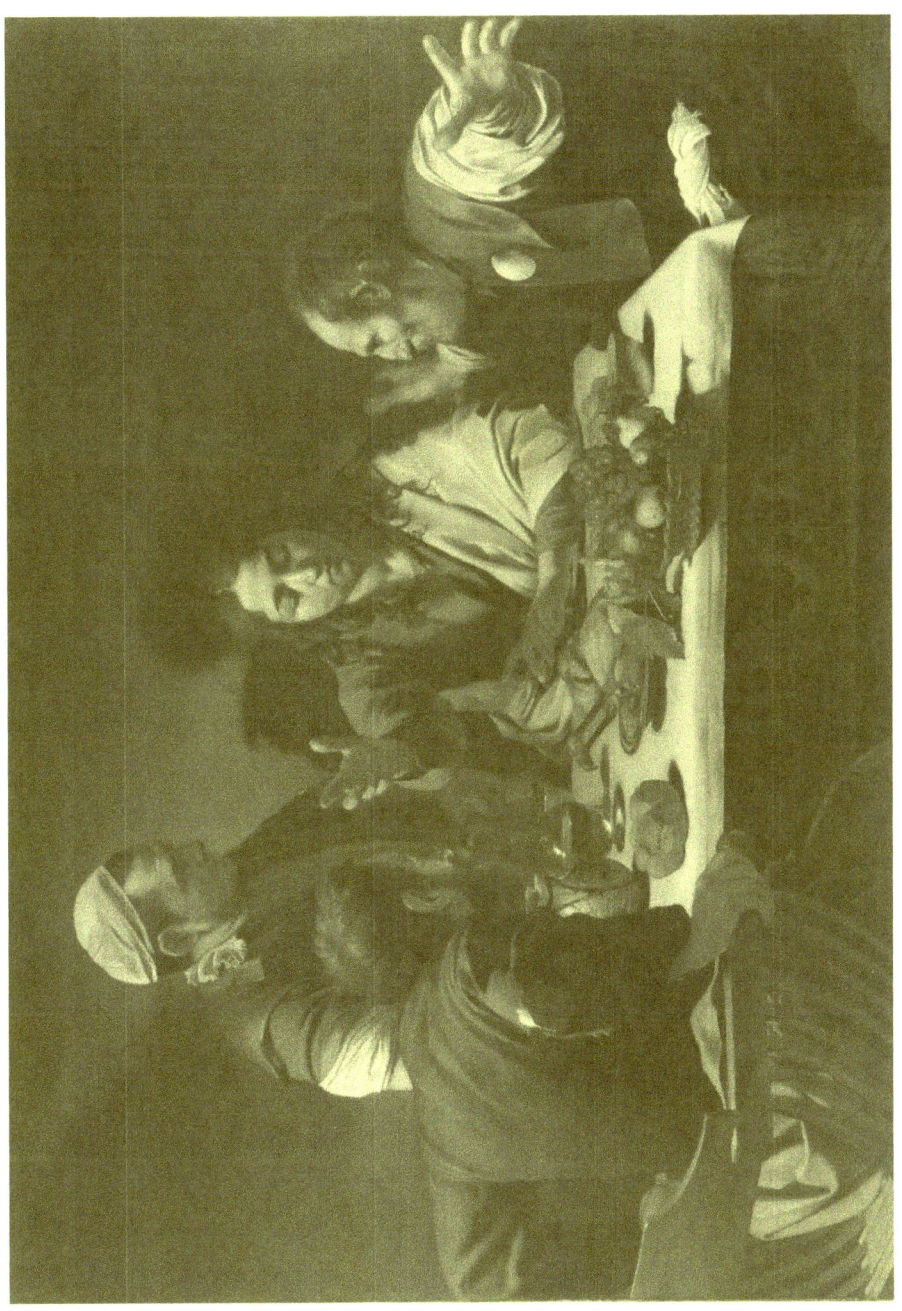

FIGURE NO. 3 ✧ Caravaggio, *Supper at Emmaus*, 1602

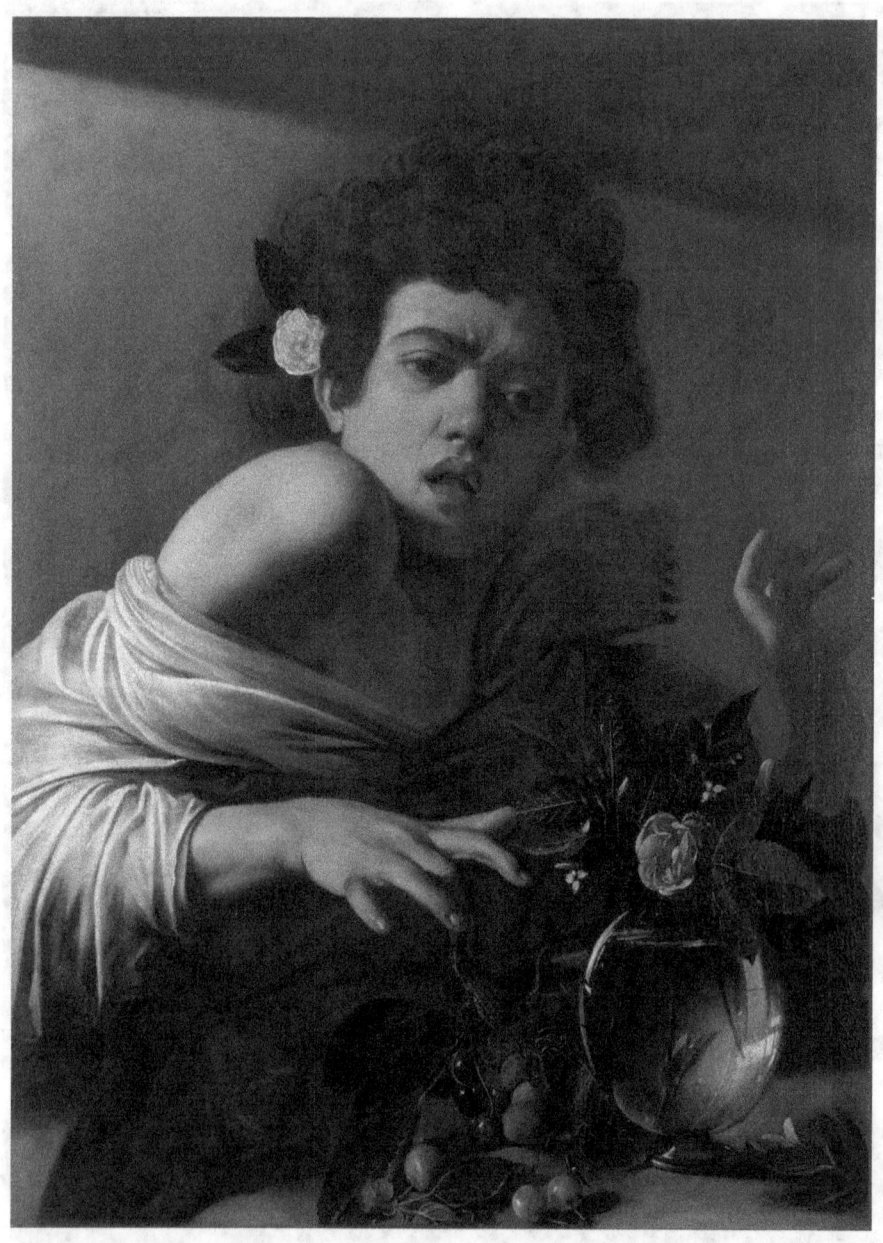

FIGURE NO. 4 ✦ Caravaggio, *Boy Bitten by a Lizard*, c. 1596

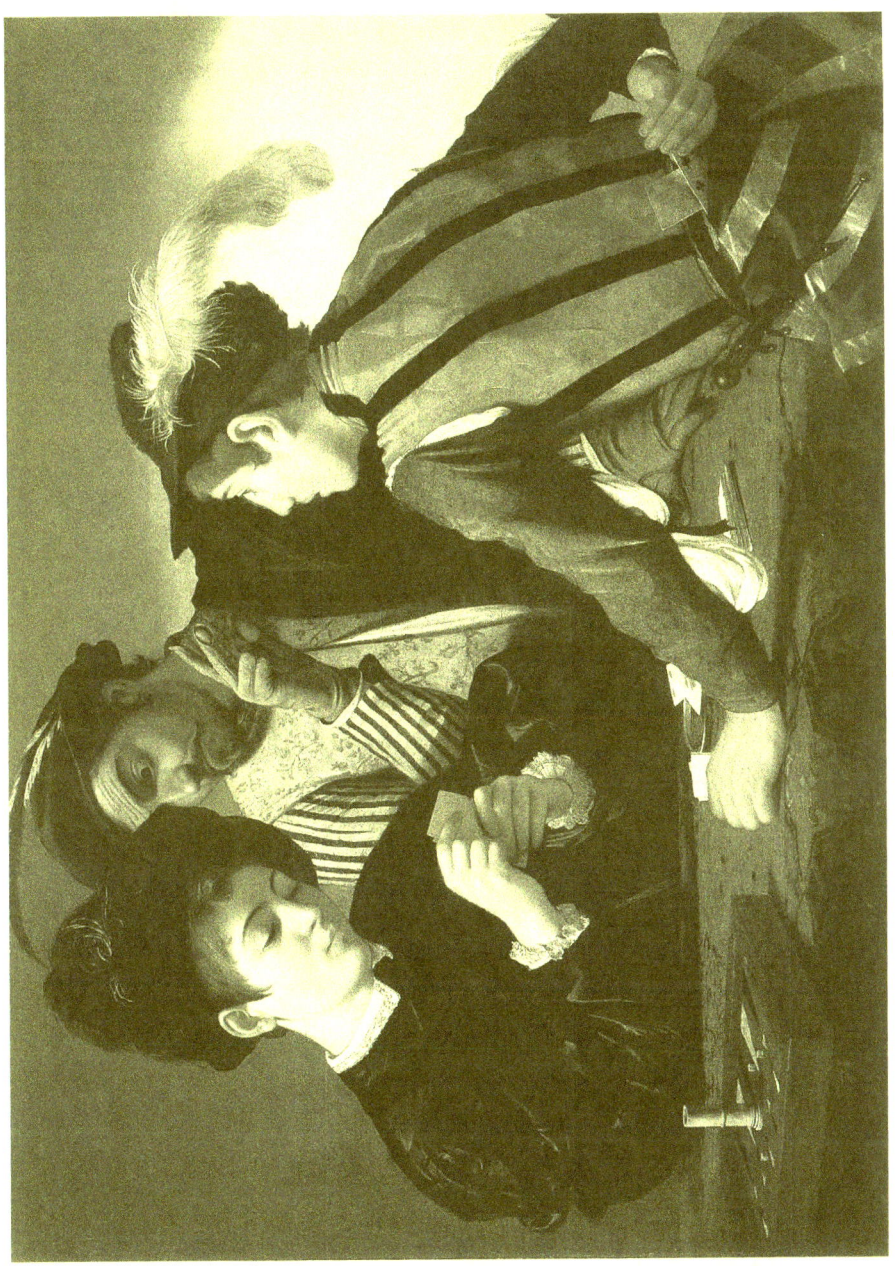

FIGURE NO. 5 ✦ Caravaggio, *The Cardsharps*, c. 1594

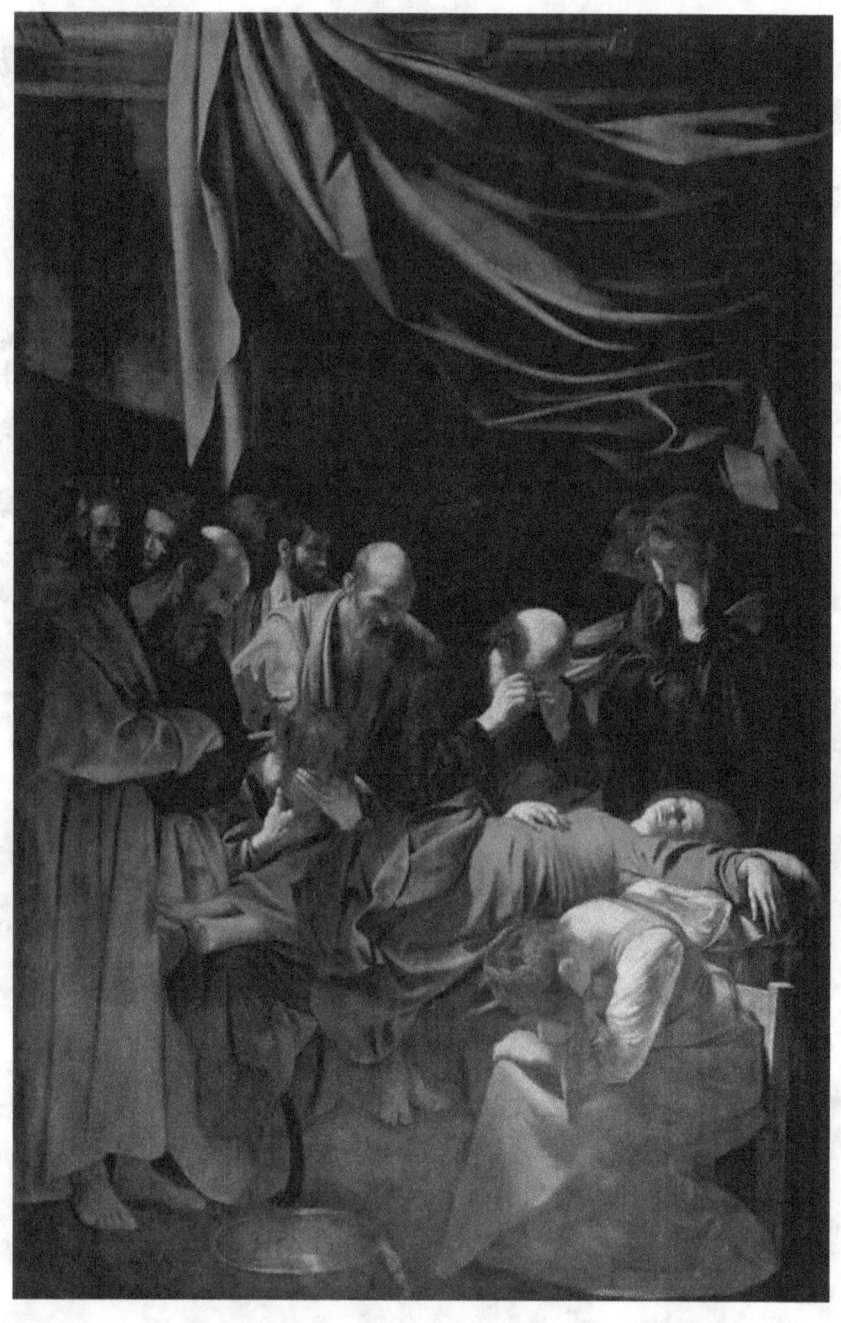

FIGURE NO. 6 ✦ Caravaggio, *Death of the Virgin*, 1601–6

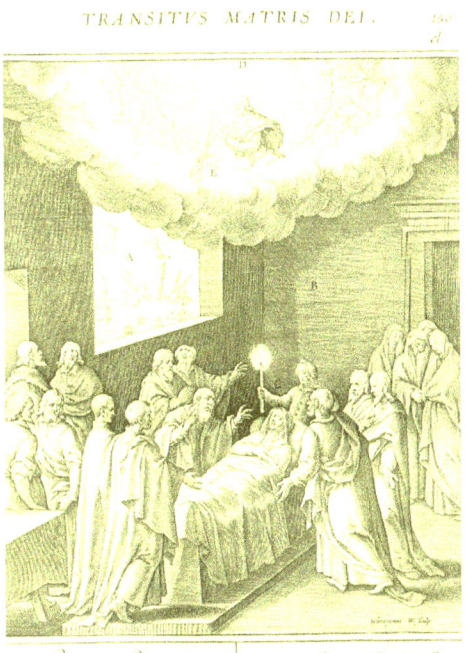

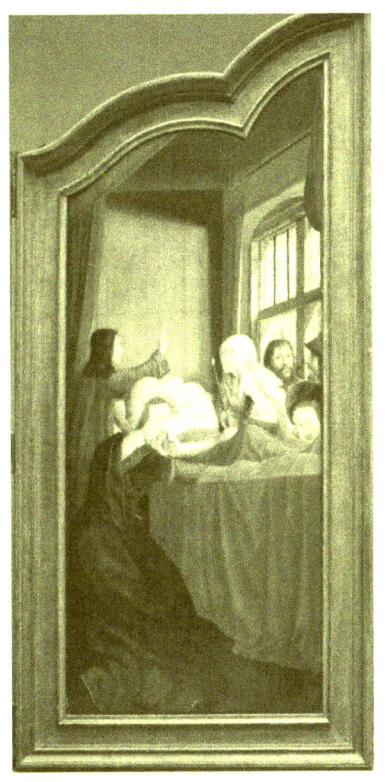

FIGURE NO. 7 ✦
Jerome Nadal, *Death of the Virgin*, 1593

FIGURE NO. 8 ✦
Quentin Massys, *Death of Saint Anne, St. Anne Altarpiece,* 1509

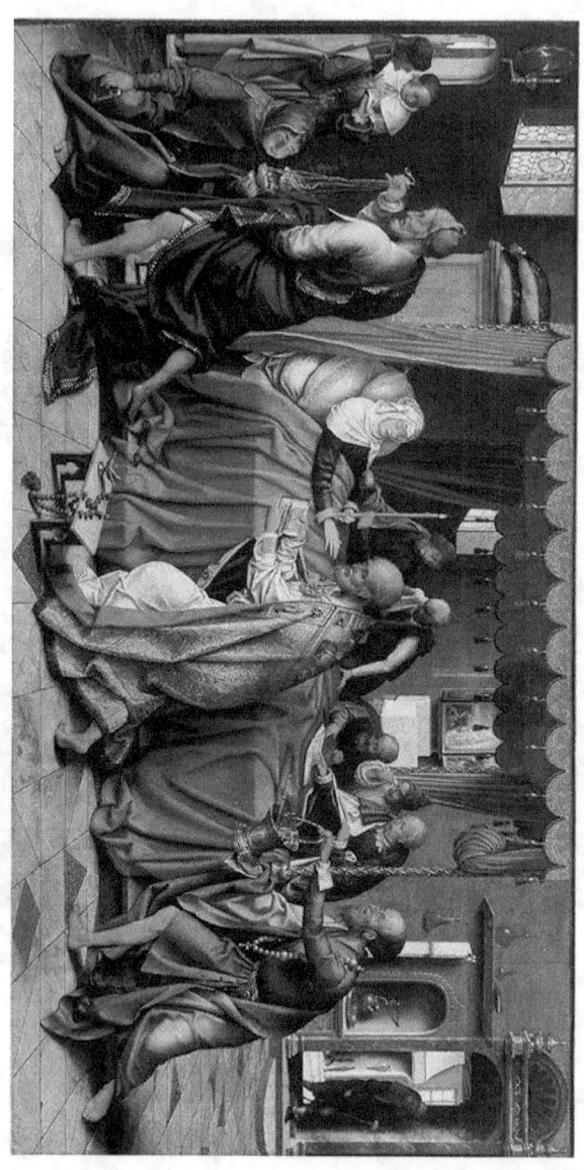

FIGURE NO. 9 ✦ Joos van Cleve, *Death of the Virgin*, c. 1515

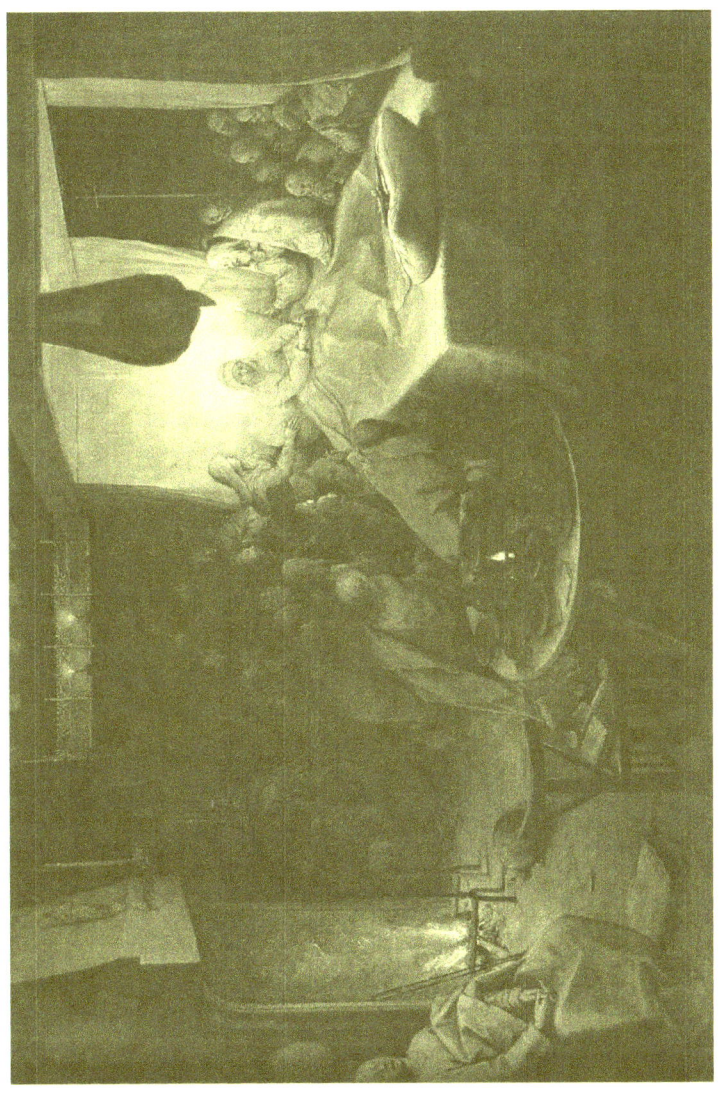

FIGURE NO. 10 ✤ Peter Breugel, *Death of the Virgin*, 1564

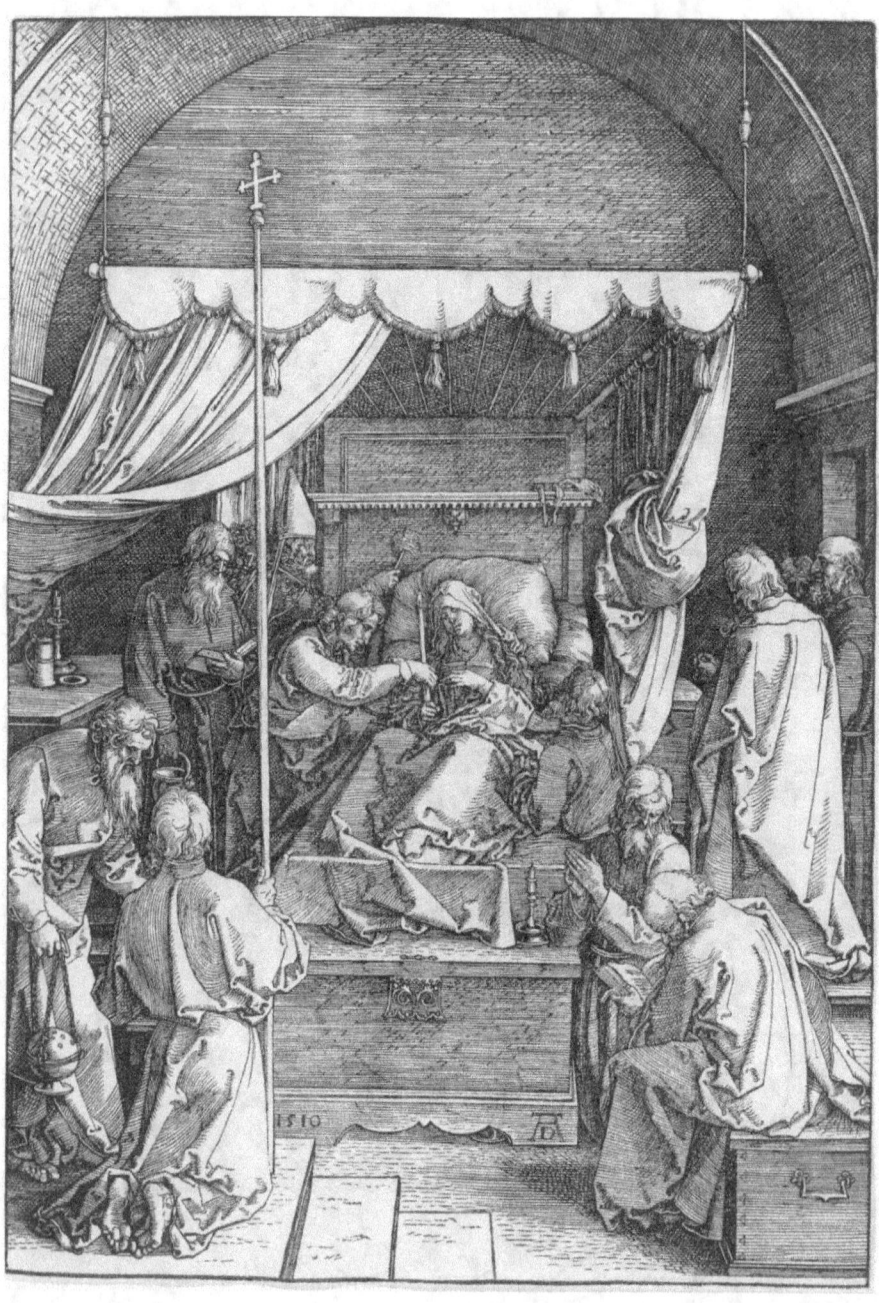

FIGURE NO. 11 ✦ Albert Dürer, *Death of the Virgin*, 1510

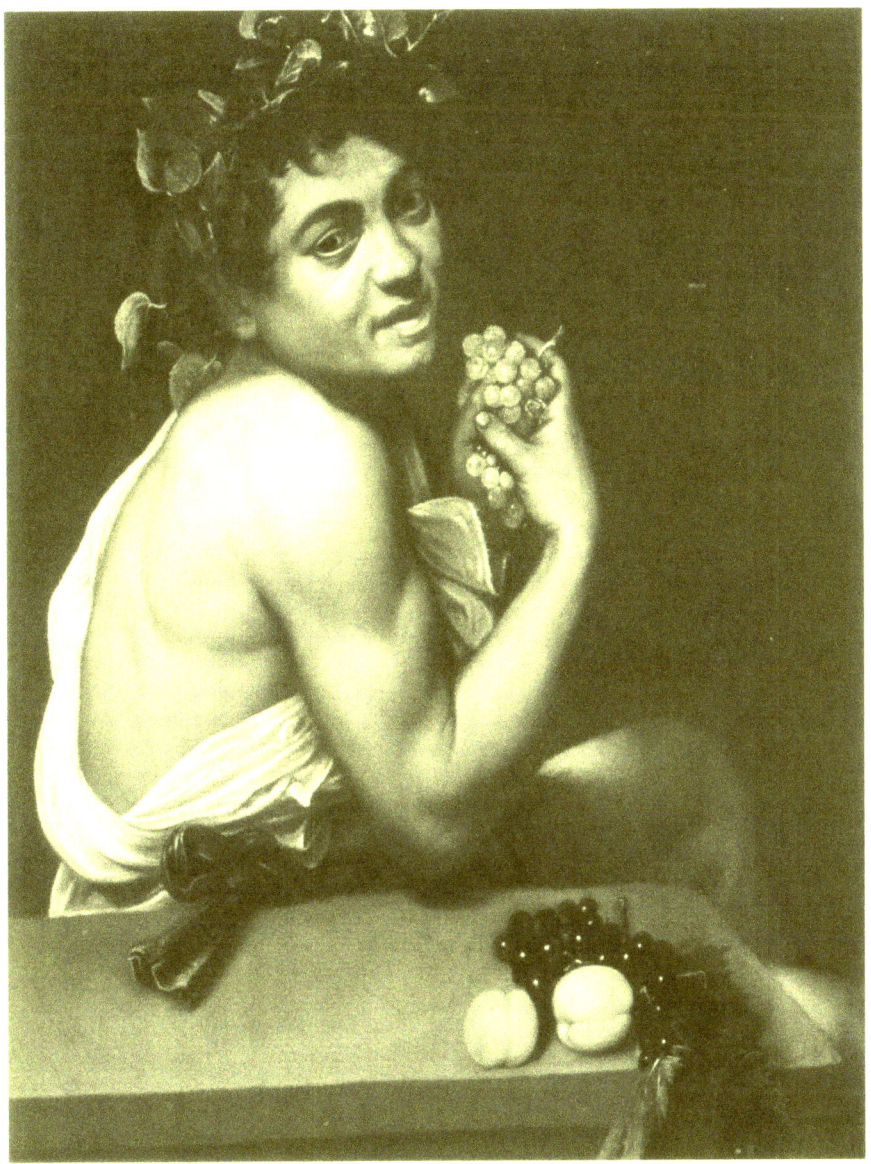

FIGURE NO. 12 ✦ Caravaggio, *Young Sick Bacchus, c.* 1593

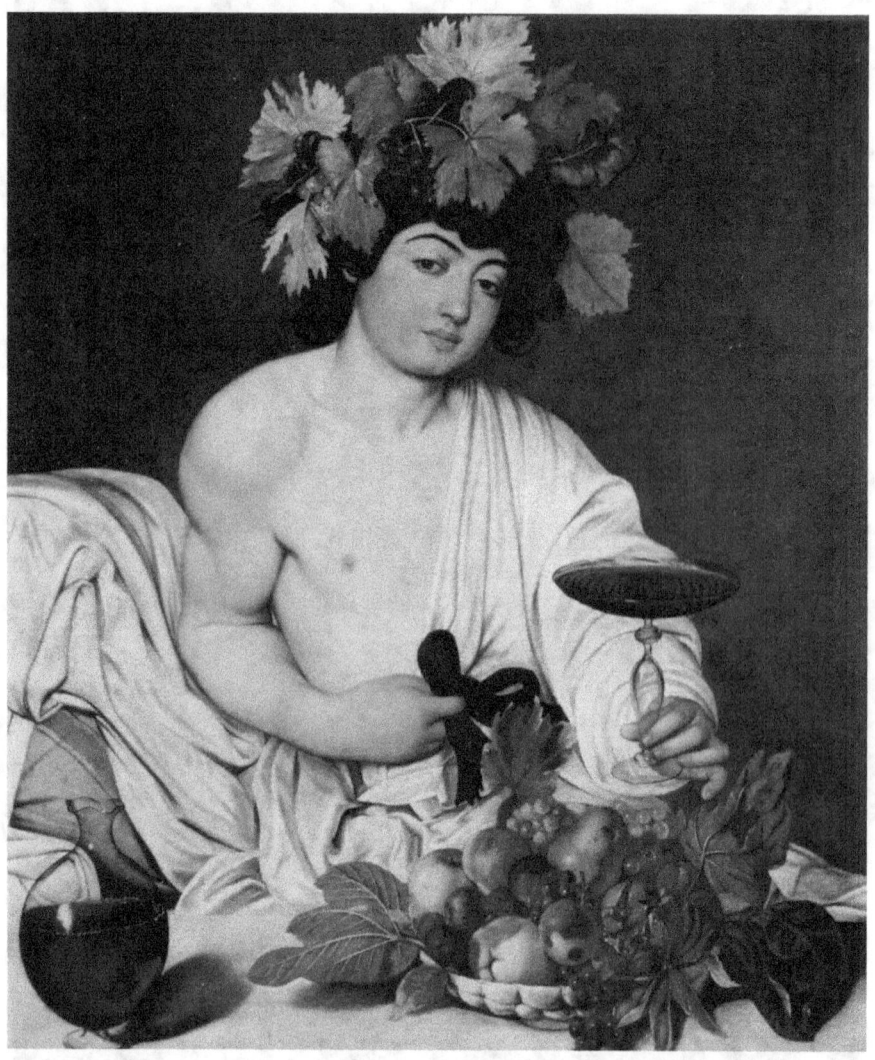

FIGURE NO. 13 ✤ Caravaggio, *Bacchus*, c. 1596

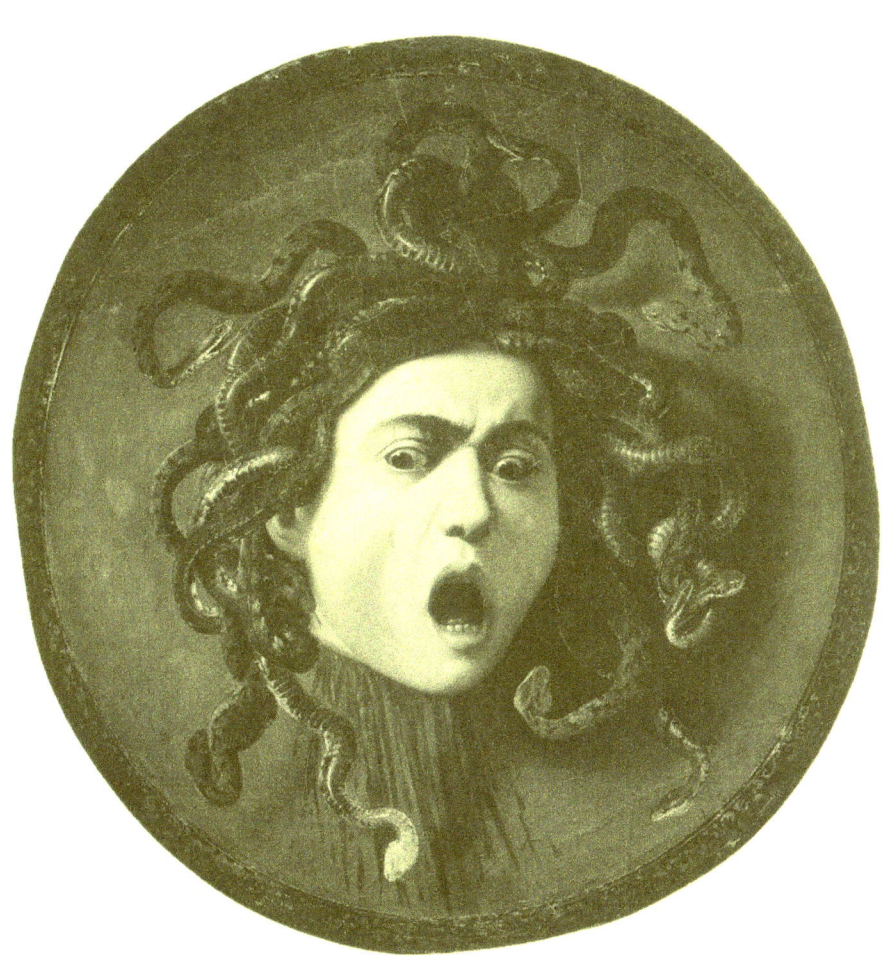

FIGURE NO. 14 ✦ Caravaggio, *Medusa*, 1597

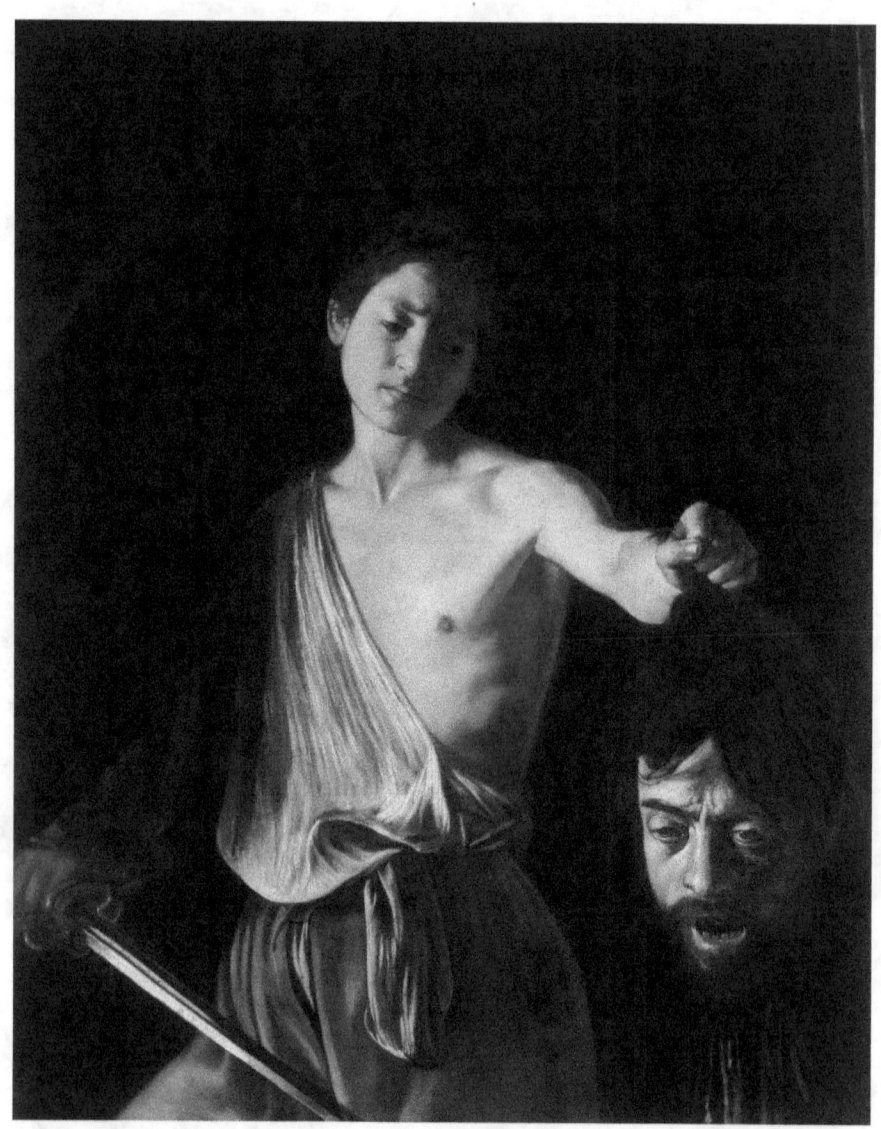

Figure no. 15 ✤ Caravaggio, *David with the Head of Goliath*, 1610

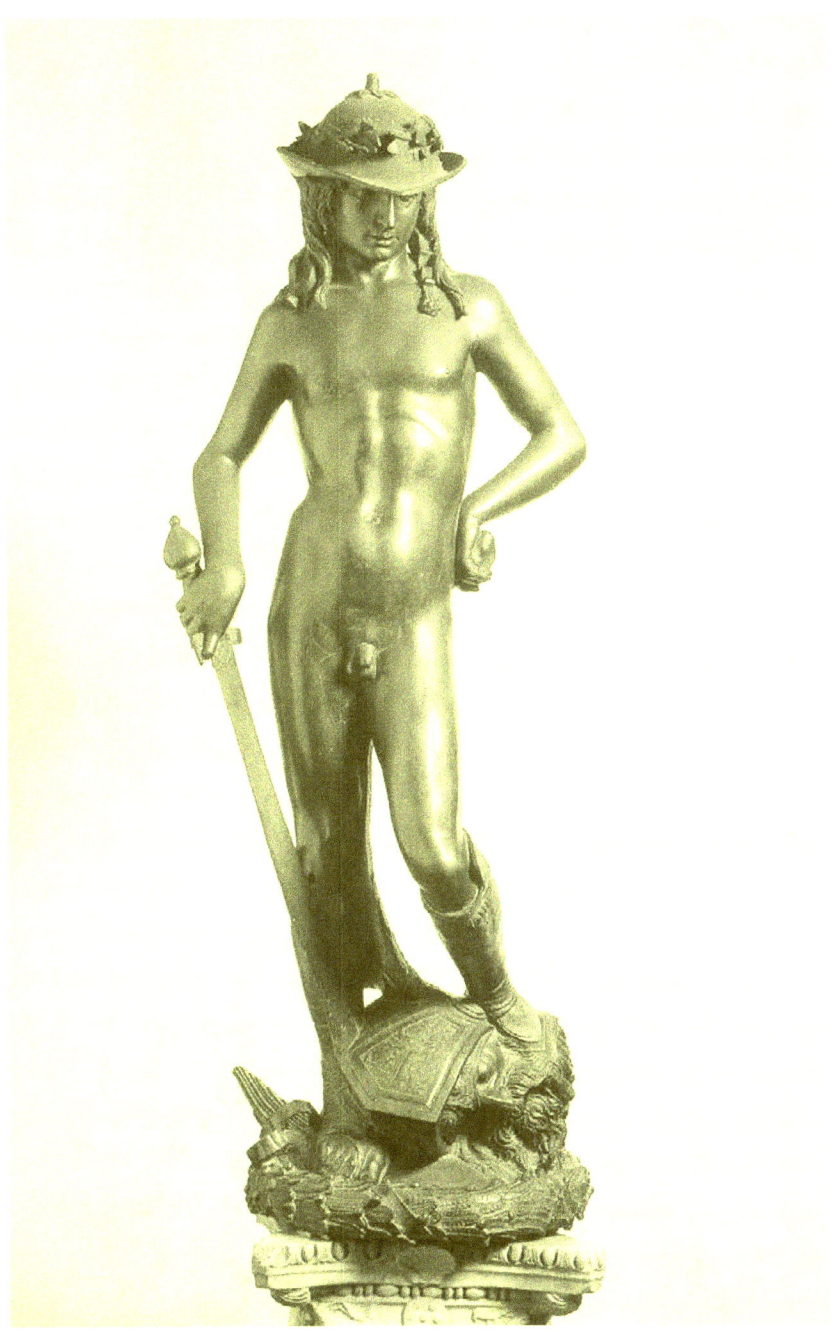

FIGURE NO. 16 ✦ Donatello, *David, c.* 1435–40

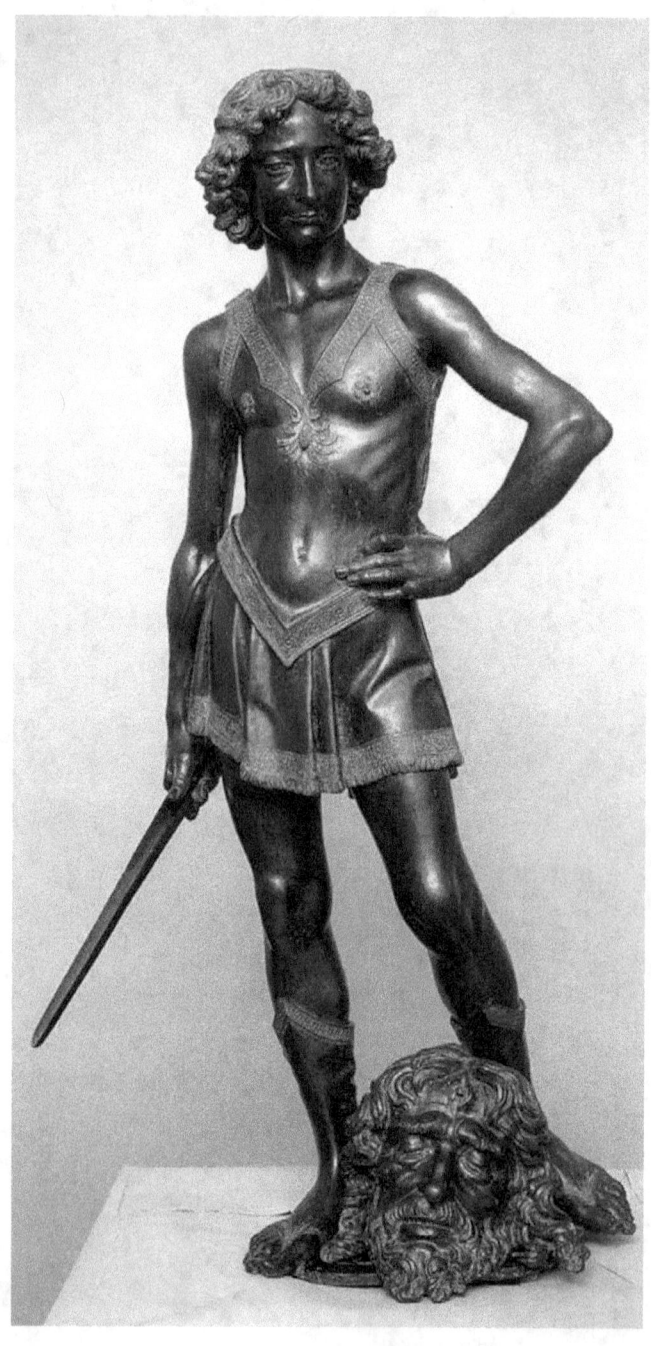

Figure no. 17 ✣ Andrea del Verrocchio, *David*, 1473–5

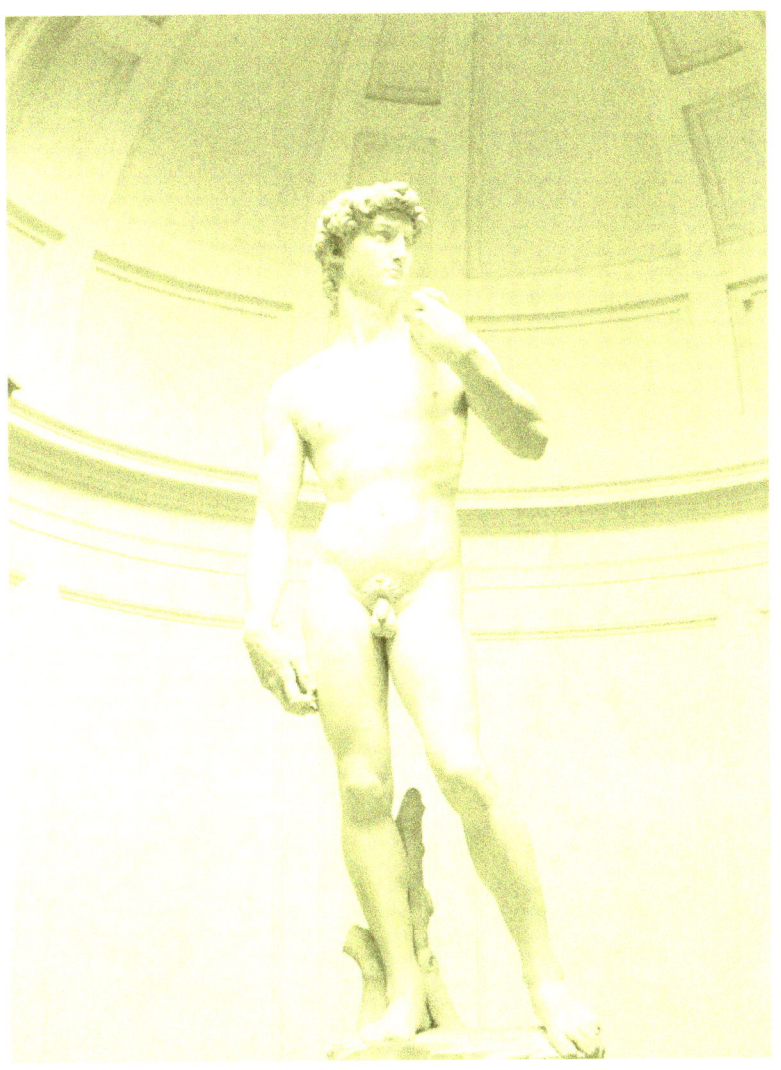

FIGURE NO. 18 ✣ Michelangelo, *David*, 1501–4

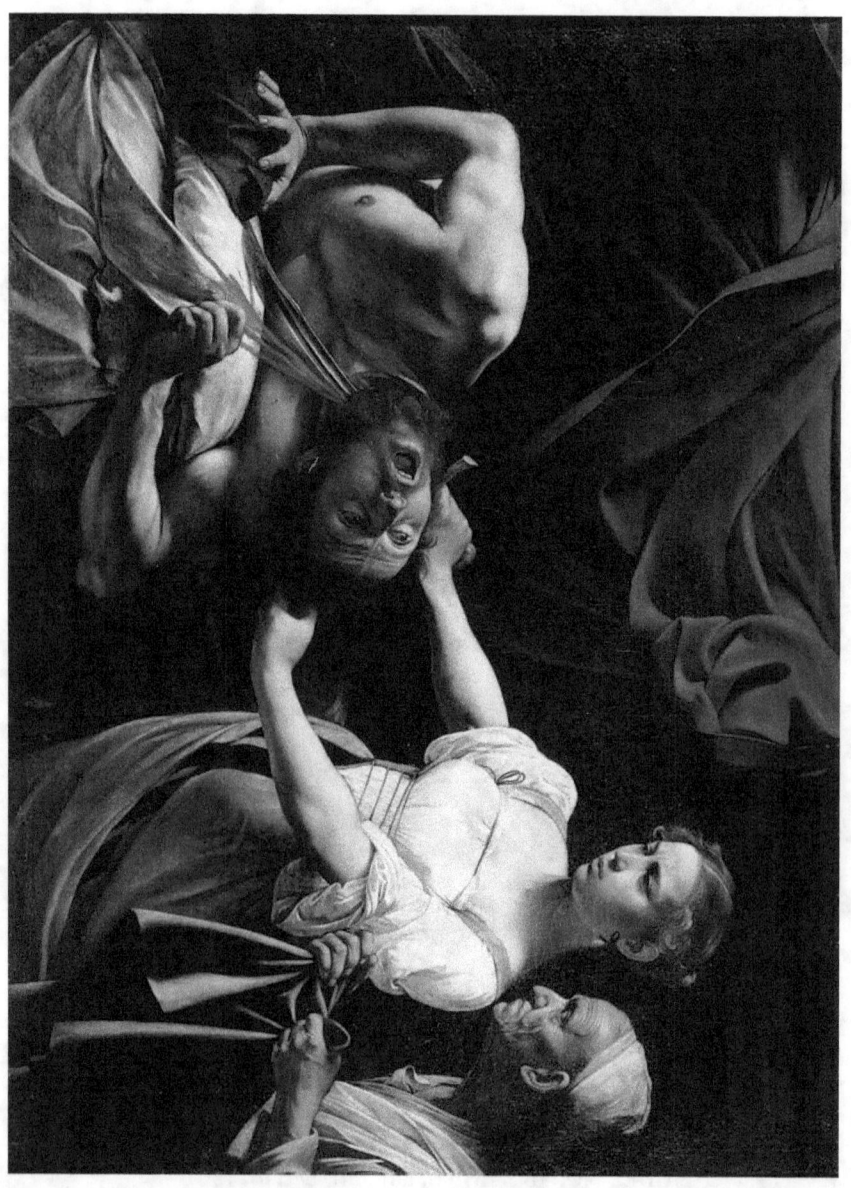

FIGURE NO. 19 ✣ Caravaggio, *Judith Beheading Holofernes*, c. 1598

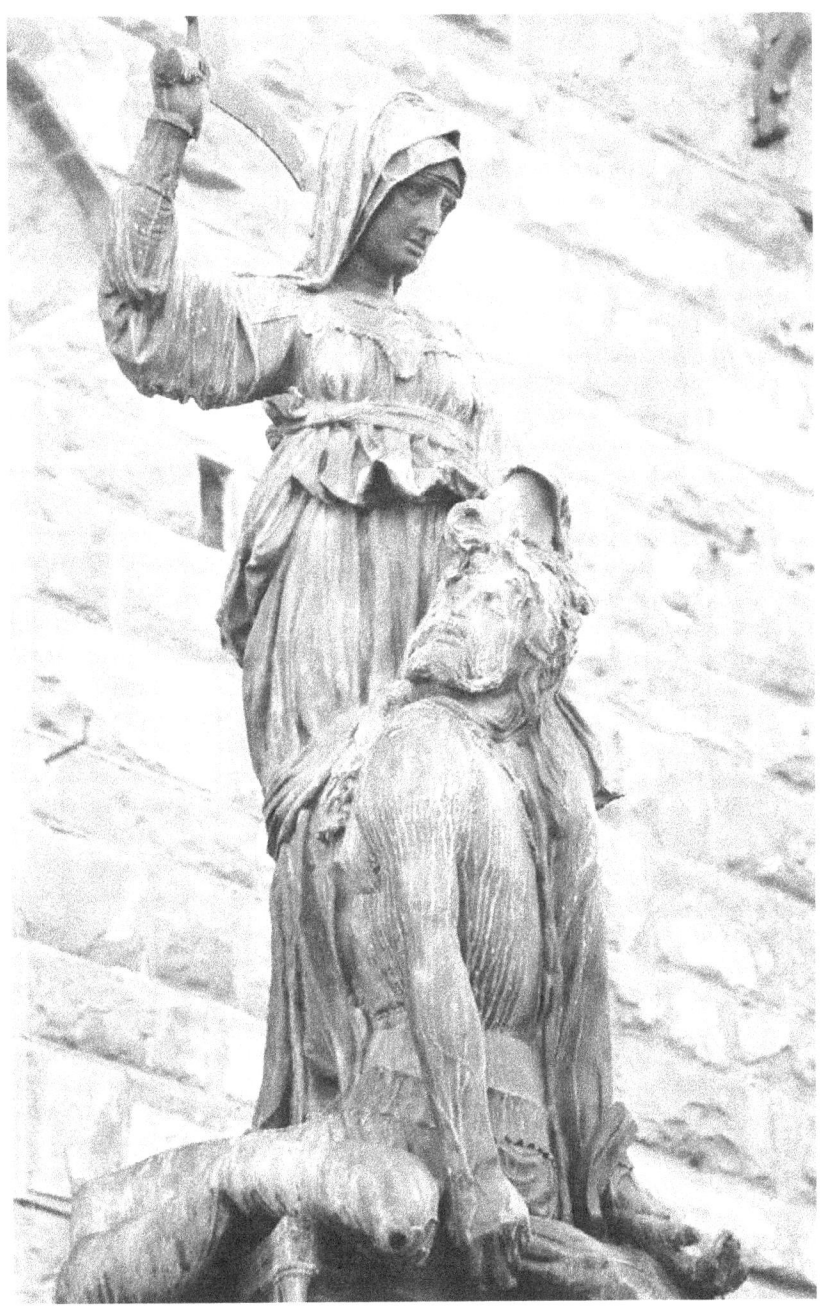

FIGURE NO. 20 ✦ Donatello, *Judith and Holofernes*, 1460

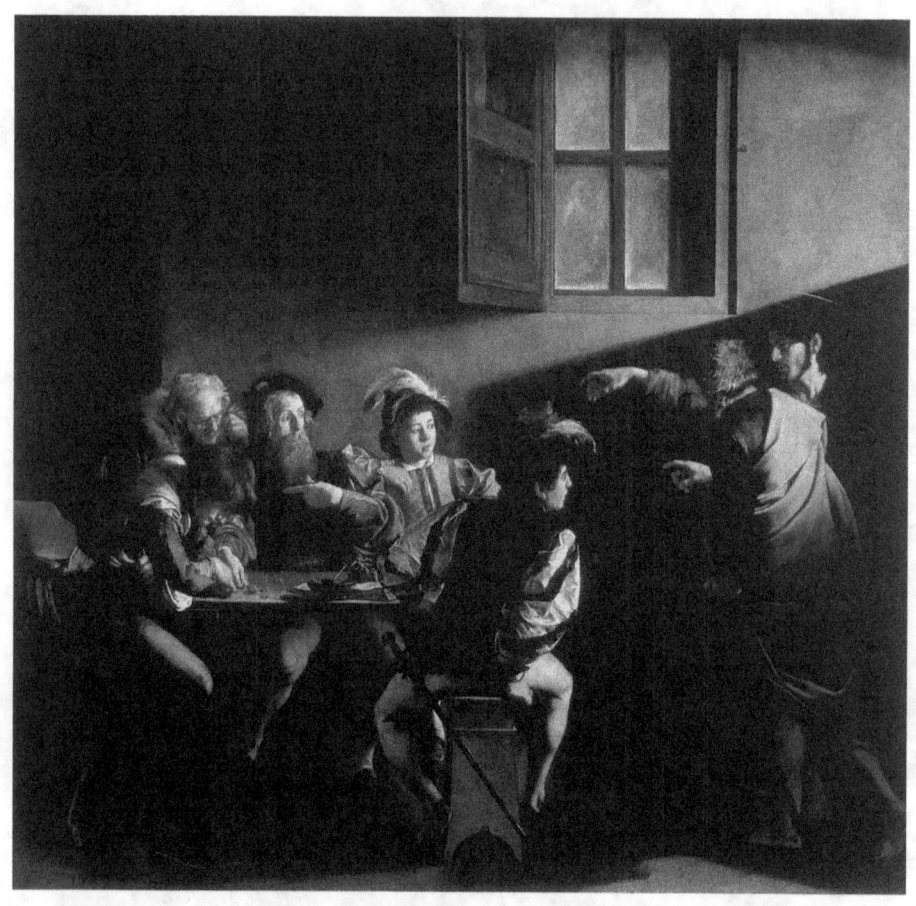

FIGURE NO. 21 ✦ Caravaggio, *Calling of Saint Matthew, c.* 1600

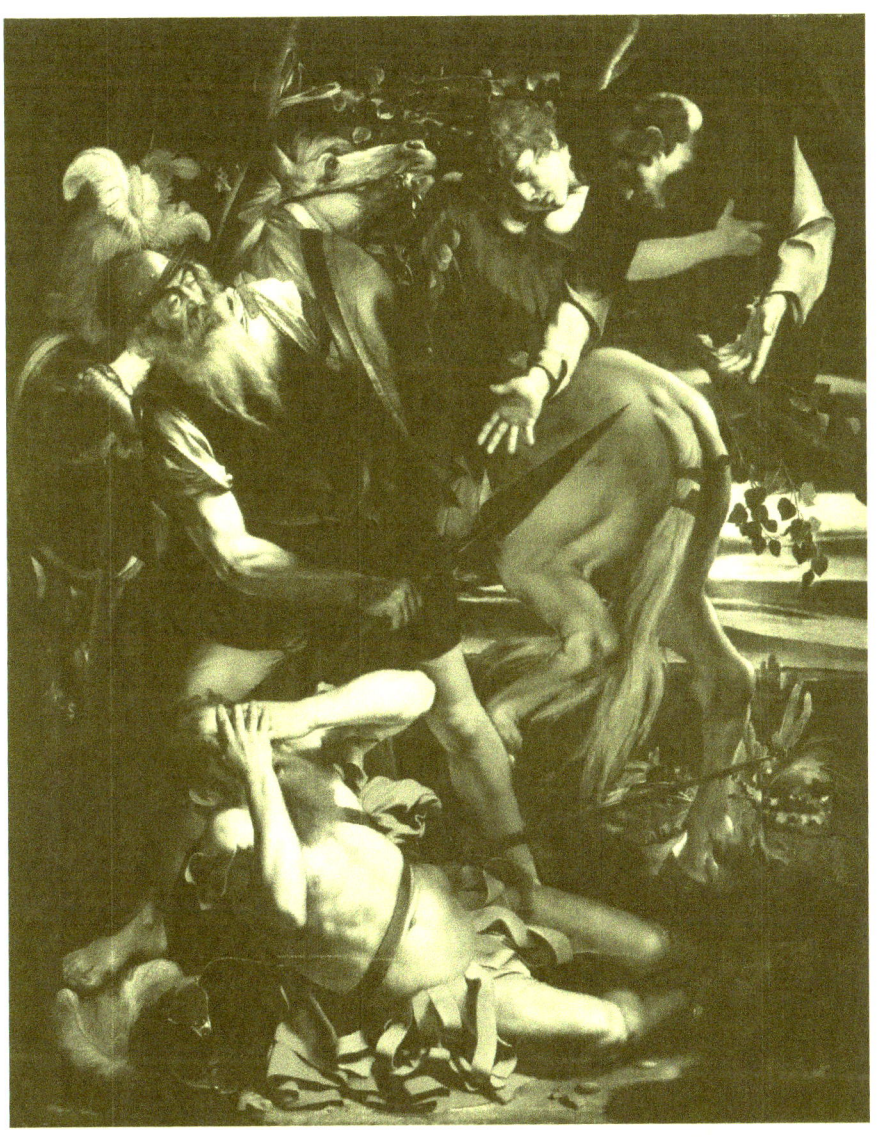

FIGURE NO. 22 ✦ Caravaggio, *Conversion of Saint Paul*, 1600

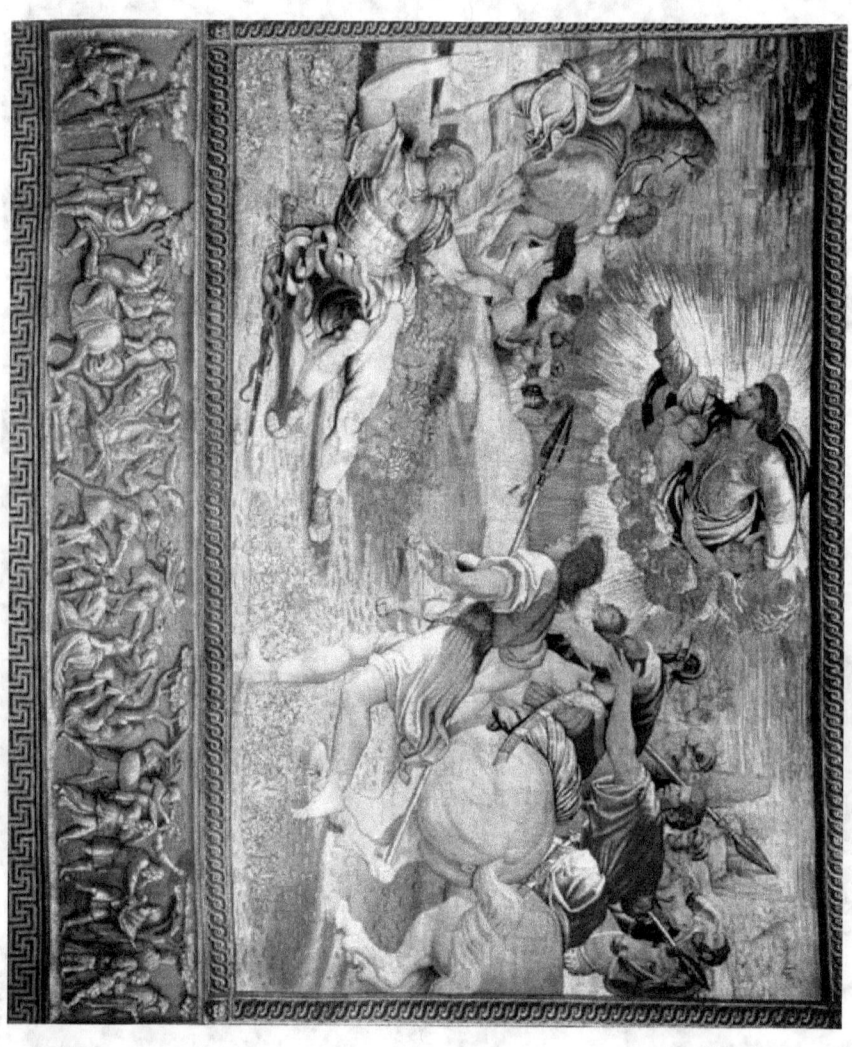

FIGURE NO. 23 ✦ Raphael, *Conversion of Saint Paul*, 1517–35

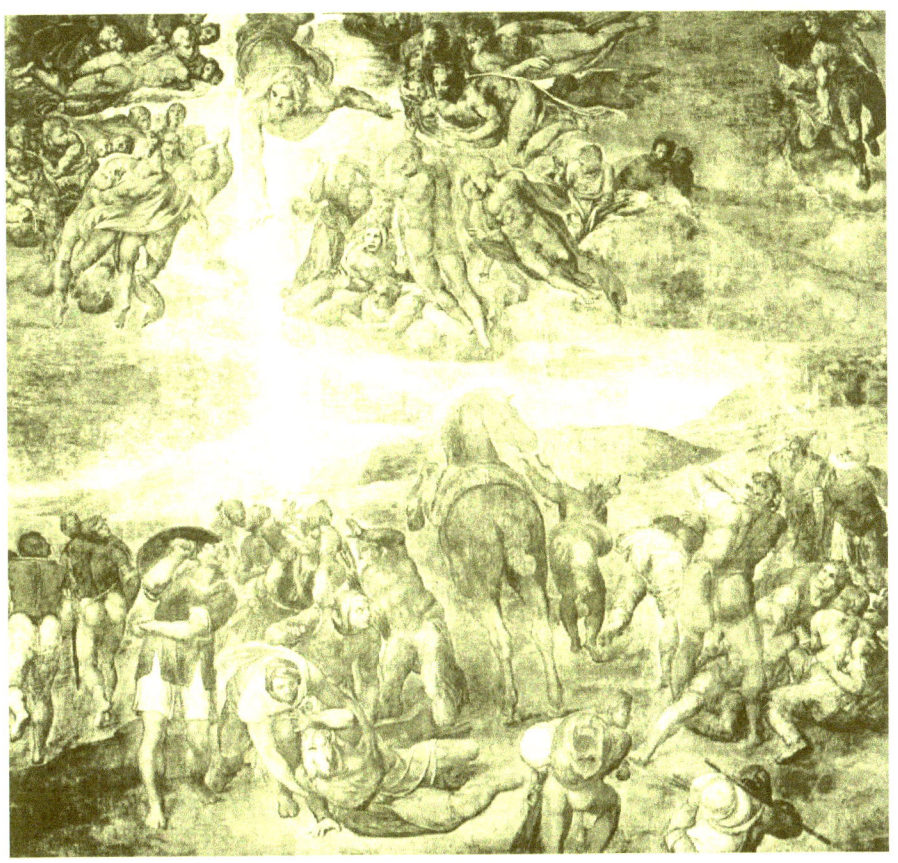

FIGURE NO. 24 ✦ Michelangelo, *Conversion of Saint Paul, c.* 1542–5

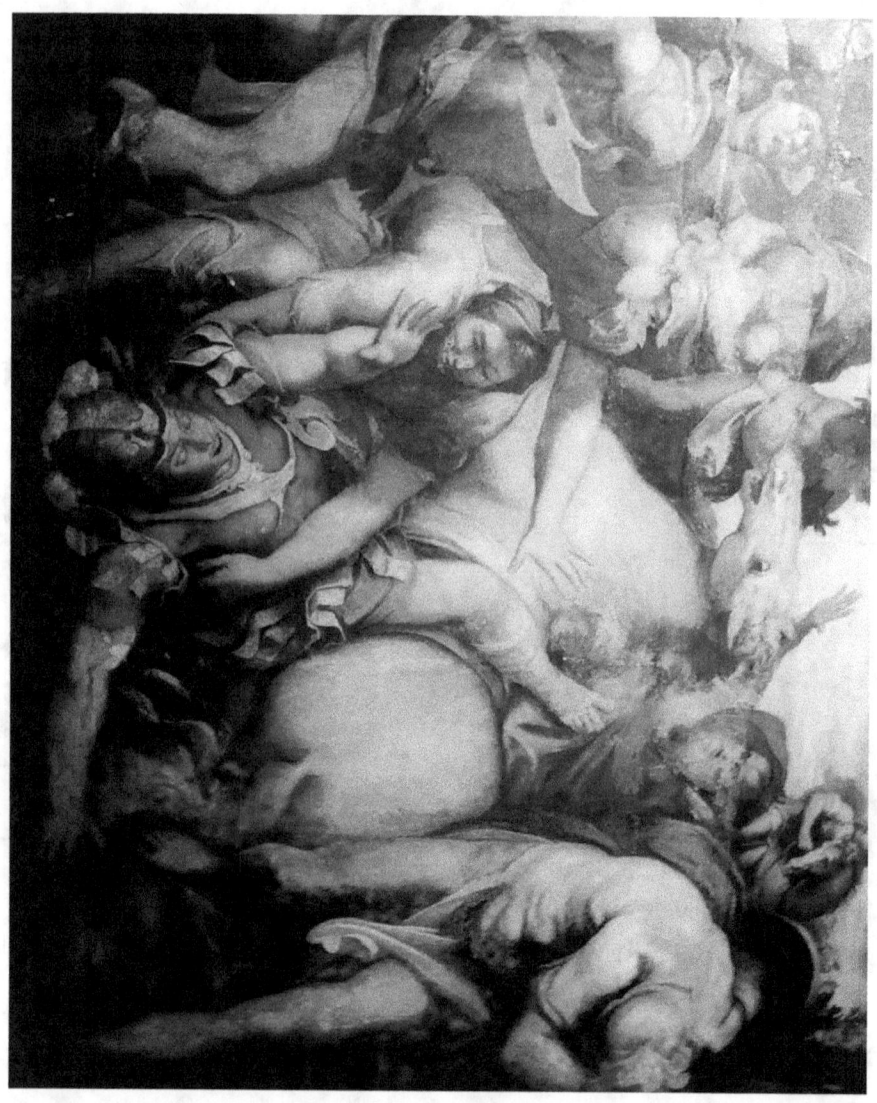

FIGURE NO. 25 ✣ Taddeo Zuccari, *Conversion of Saint Paul*, 1558

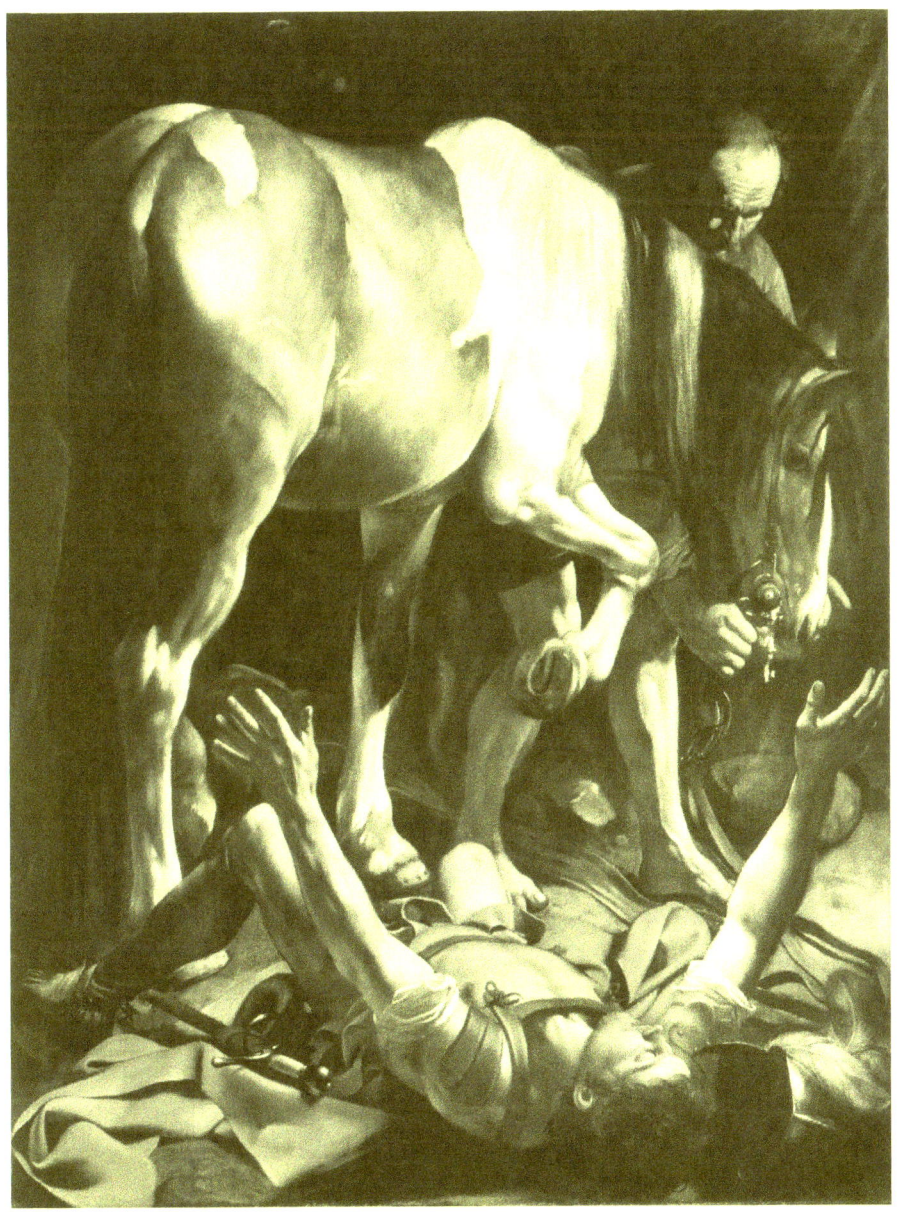

FIGURE NO. 26 ✦ Caravaggio, *Conversion on the Way to Damascus*, 1601

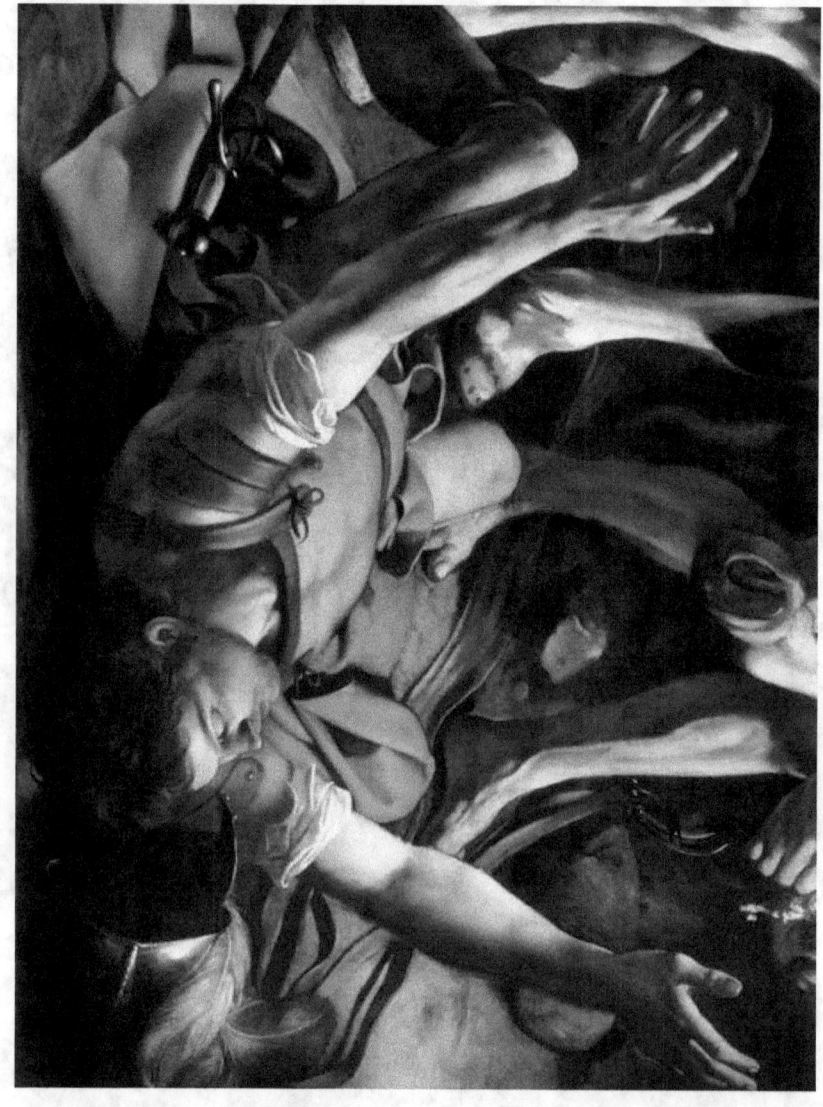

FIGURE NO. 27 ✣ Caravaggio, *Conversion on the Way to Damascus,*
detail, St. Paul

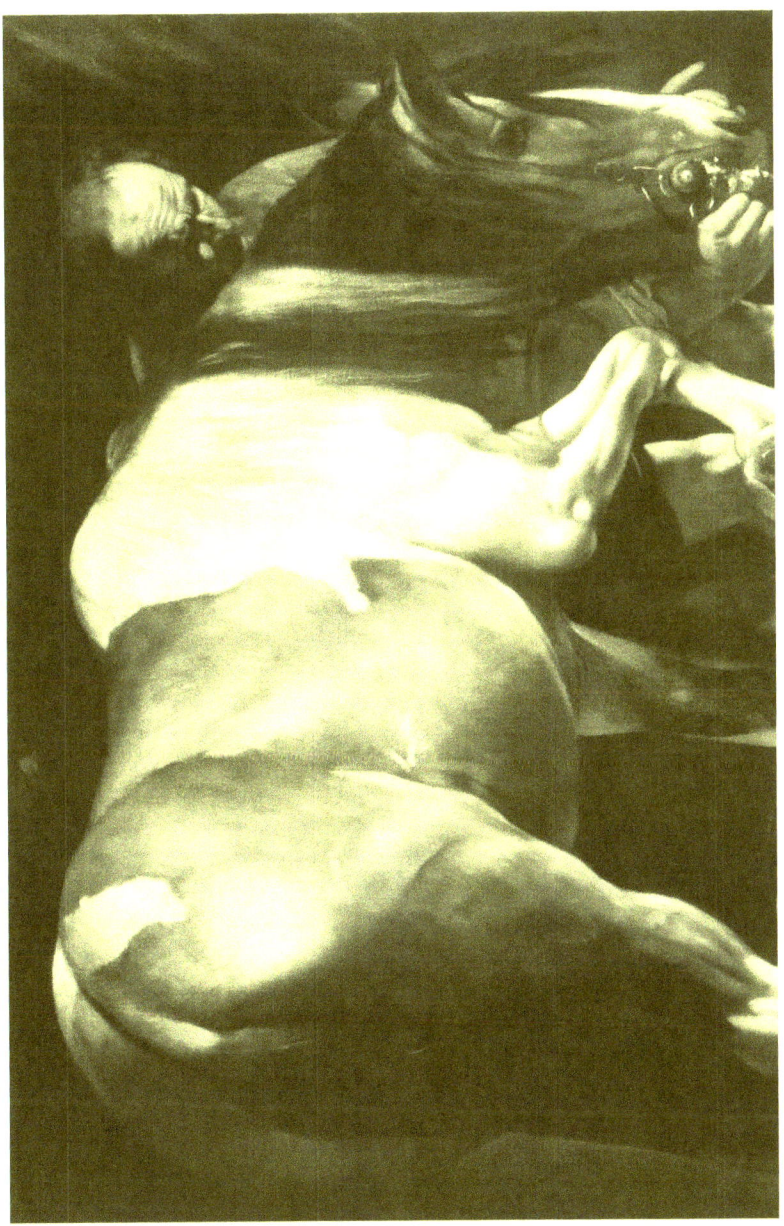

FIGURE NO. 28 ✢ Caravaggio, *Conversion on the Way to Damascus,*
detail, horse and horse-groom

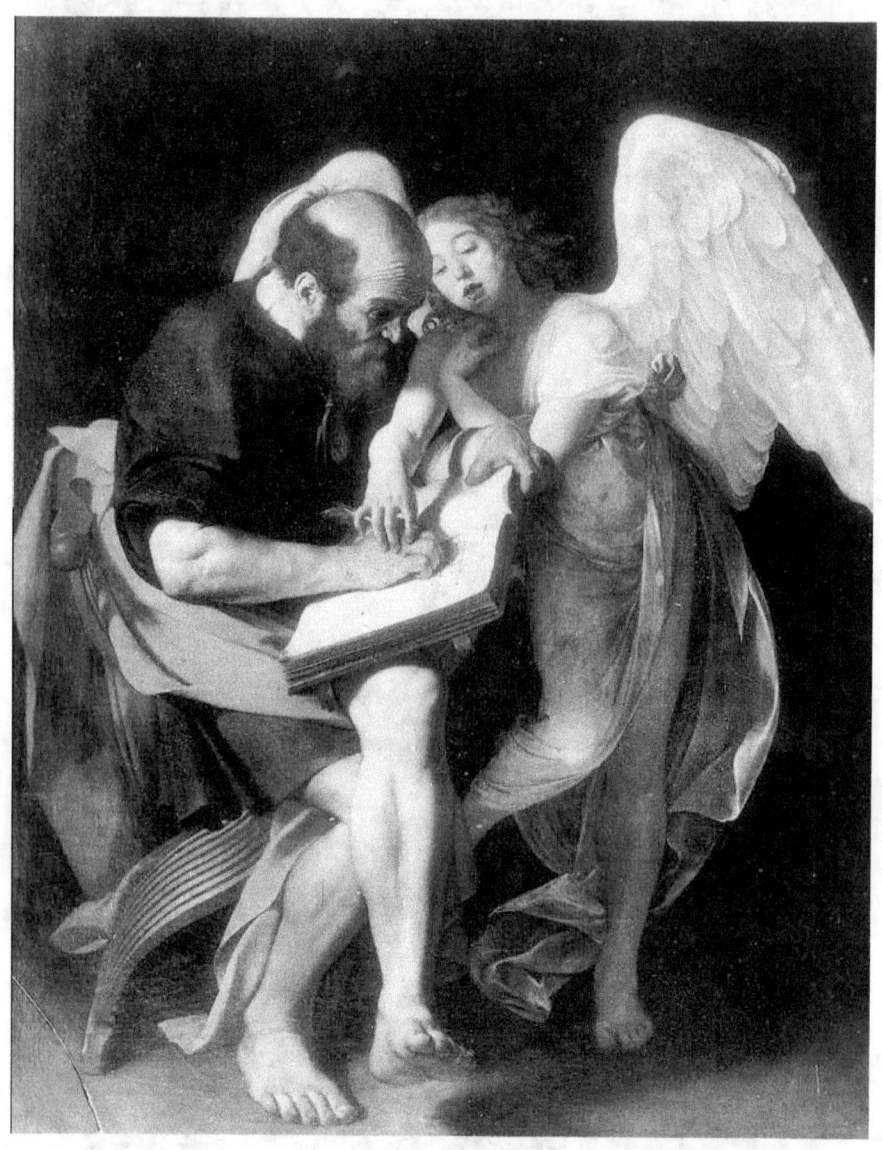

Figure no. 29 ✦ Caravaggio, *Saint Mathew and the Angel*, 1602

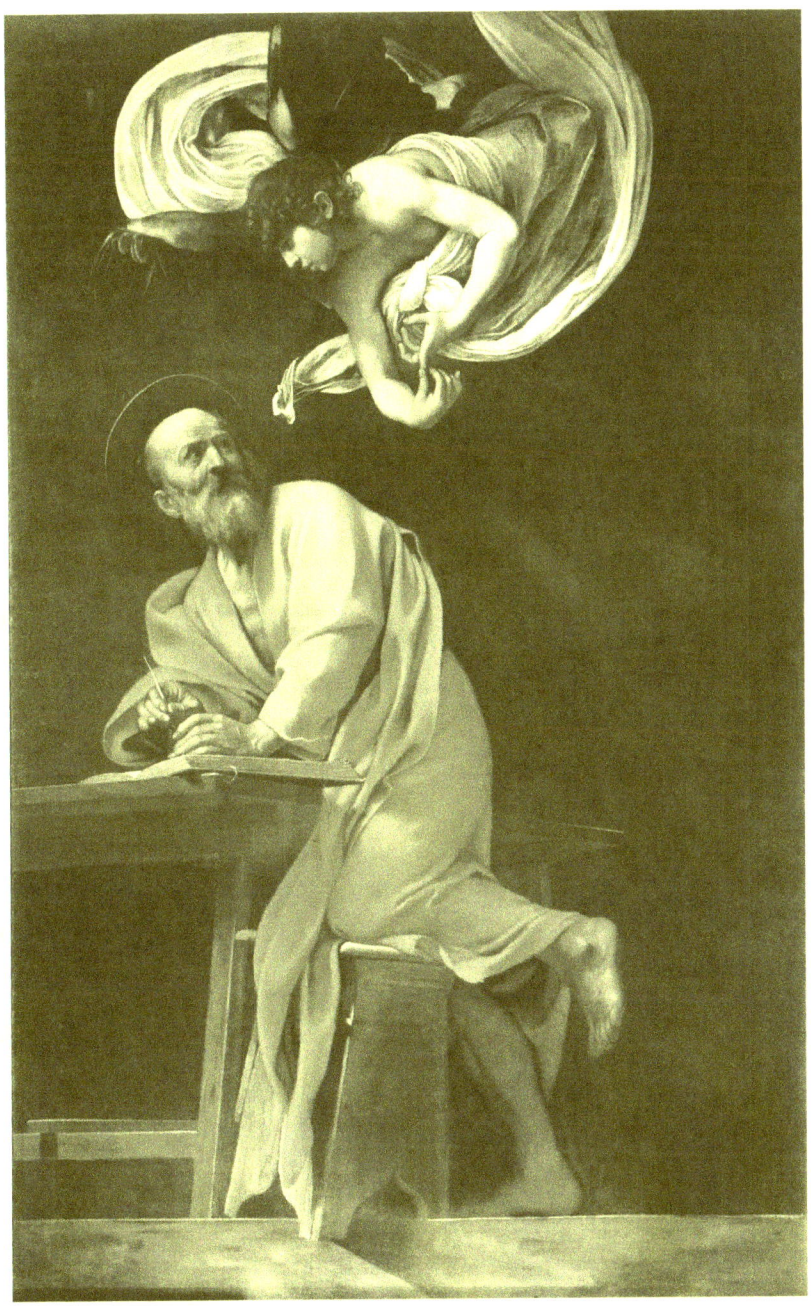

FIGURE NO. 30 ✢ Caravaggio, *Inspiration of Saint Matthew*, 1602

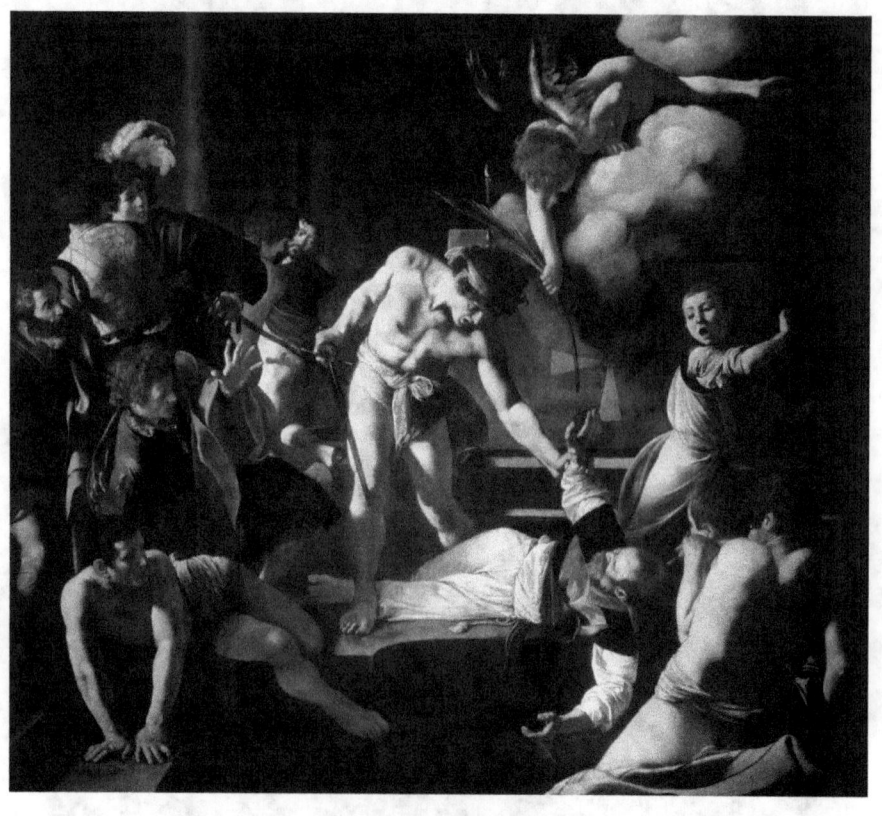

FIGURE NO. 31 ✦ Caravaggio, *Martyrdom of Saint Matthew*, 1600

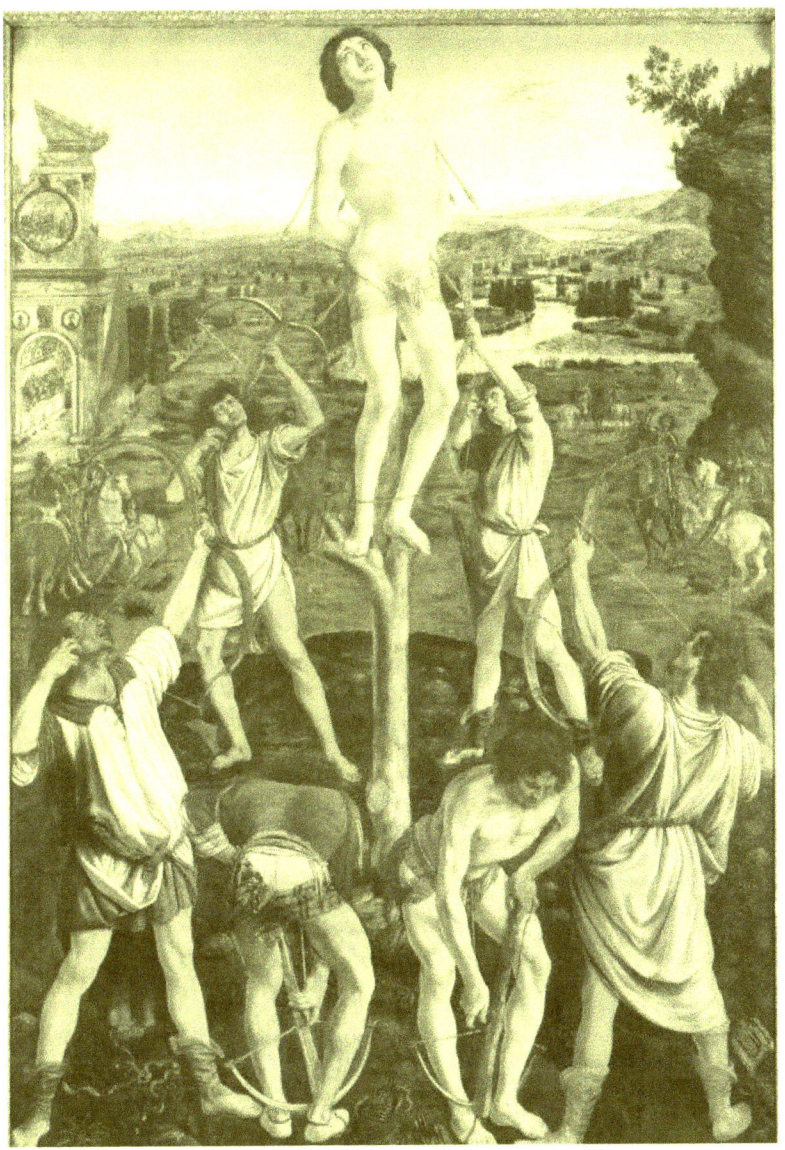

FIGURE NO. 32 ✢ Piero del Pollaiuolo, *Martyrdom of Saint Sebastian*, c. 1475

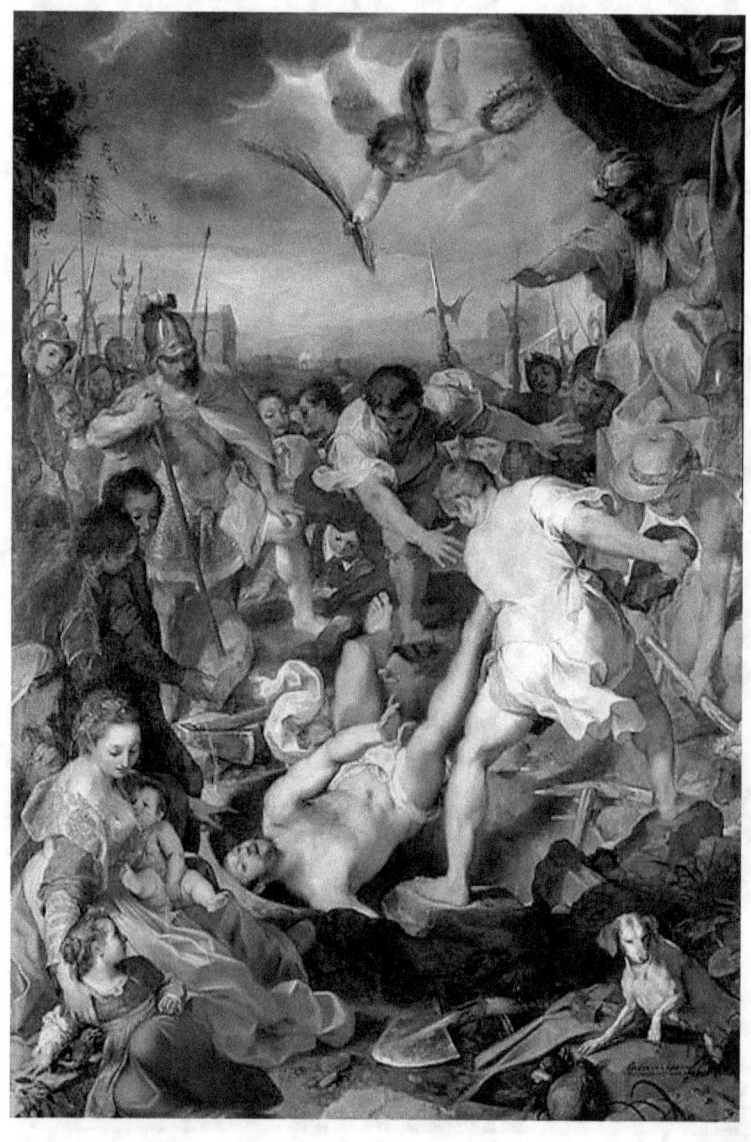

FIGURE NO. 33 ✦ Federico Barocci, *Martyrdom of Saint Vitale*, 1583

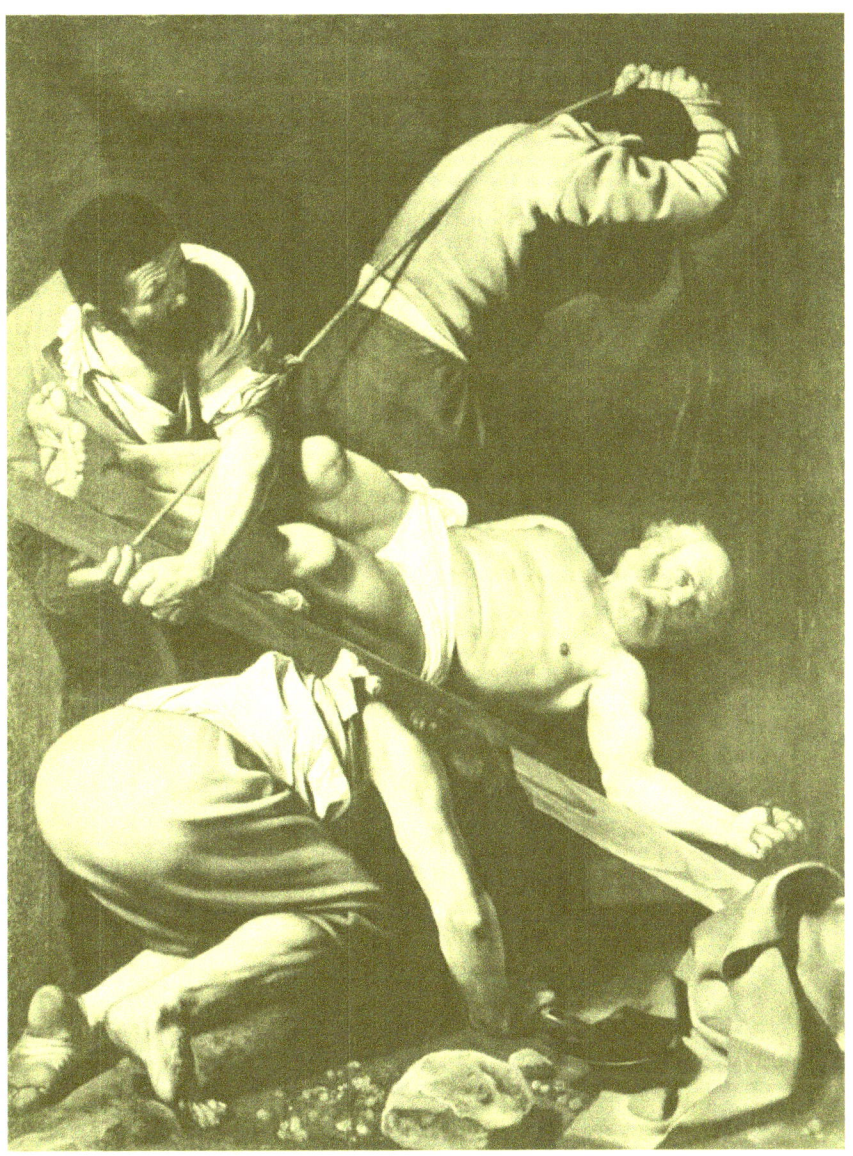

FIGURE NO. 34 ✢ Caravaggio, *Crucifixion of Saint Peter*, 1601

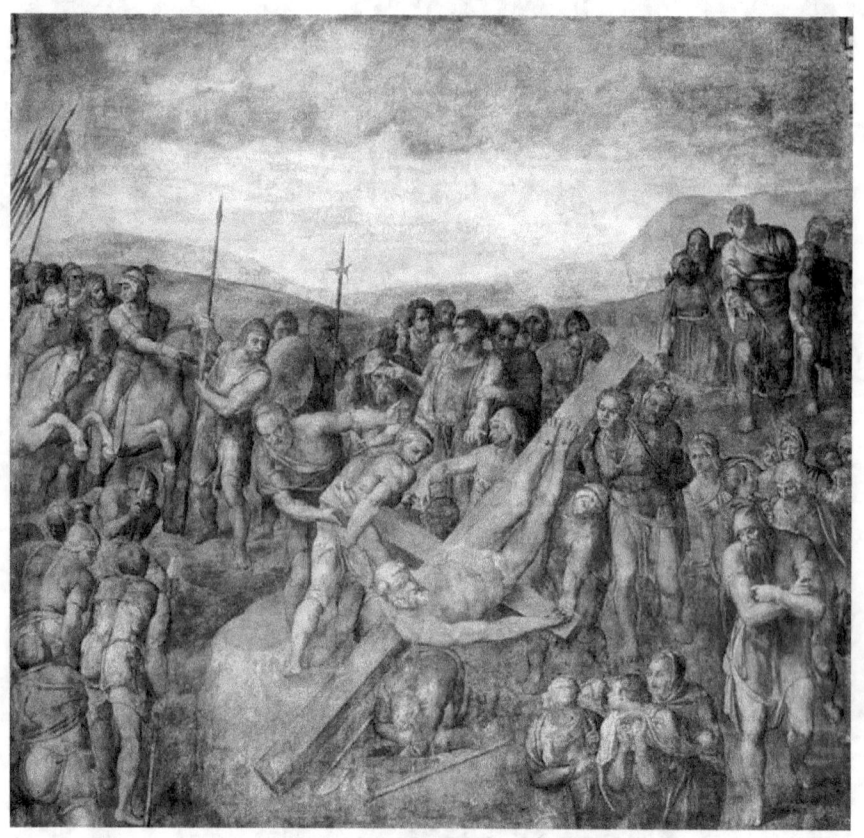

FIGURE NO. 35 ✤ Michelangelo, *Crucifixion of Saint Peter*, c. 1546–50

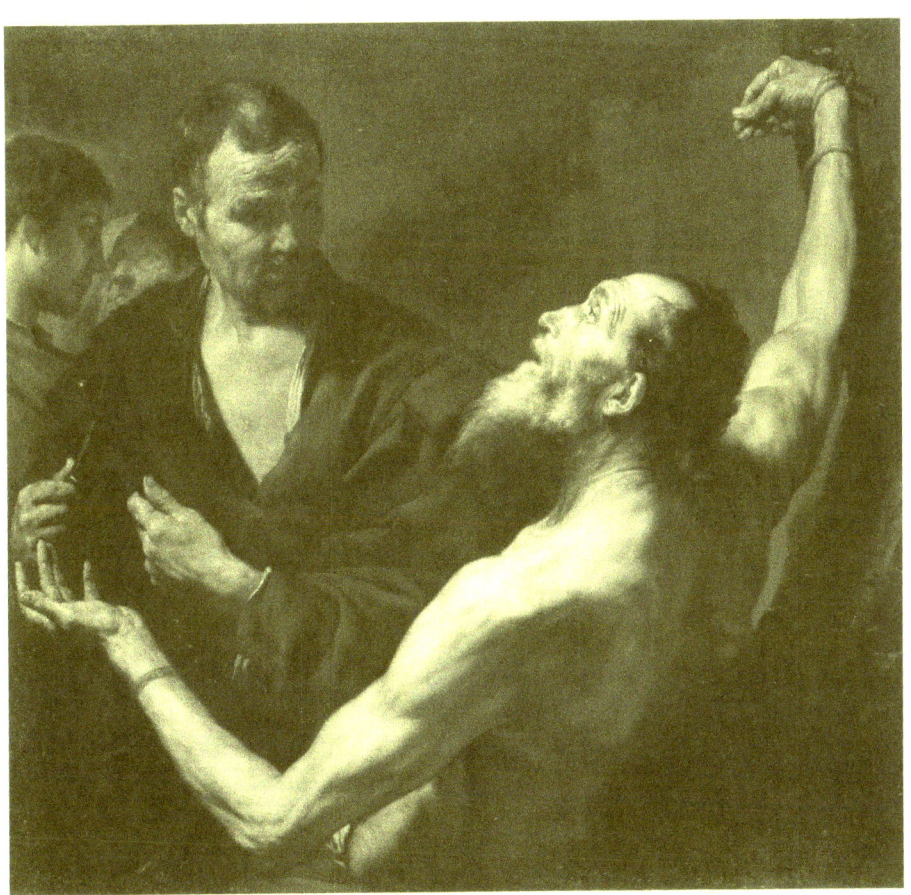

FIGURE NO. 36 ✥ José de Ribera, *Martyrdom of Saint Bartholomew*, 1634

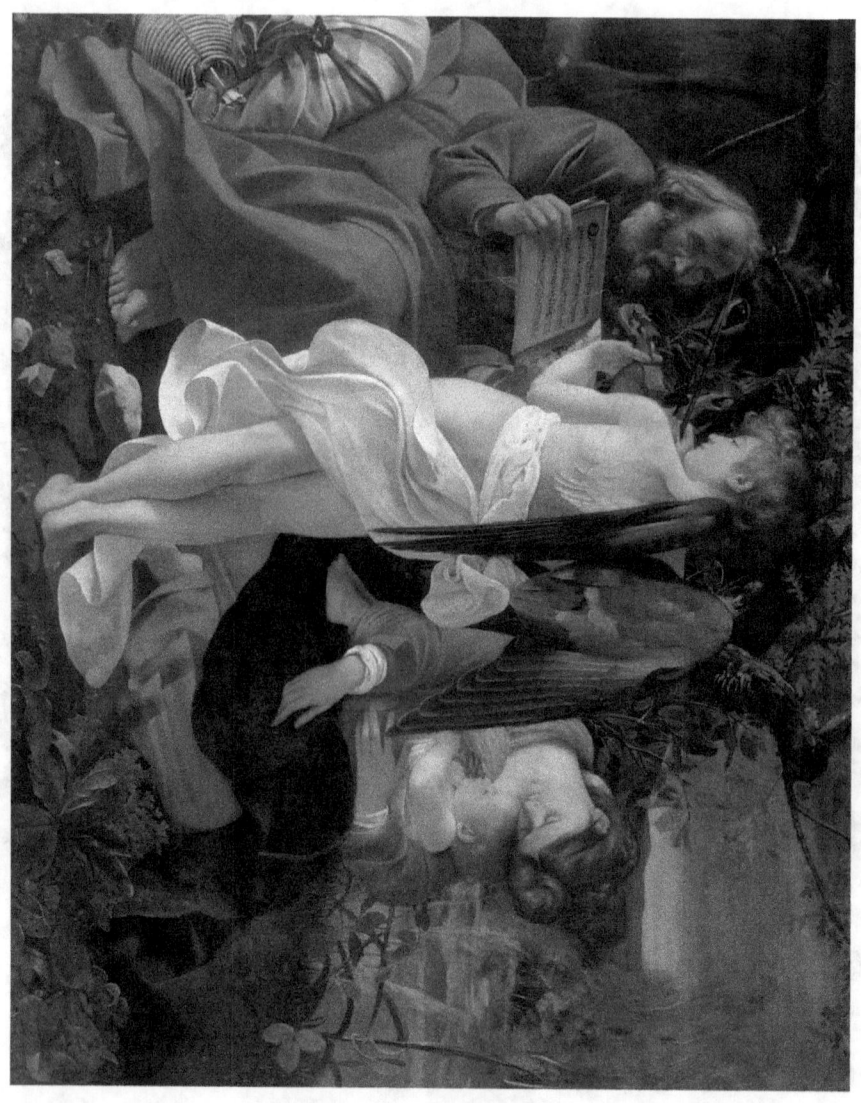

FIGURE NO. 37 ⊕ Caravaggio, *Rest on Flight to Egypt, c.* 1597

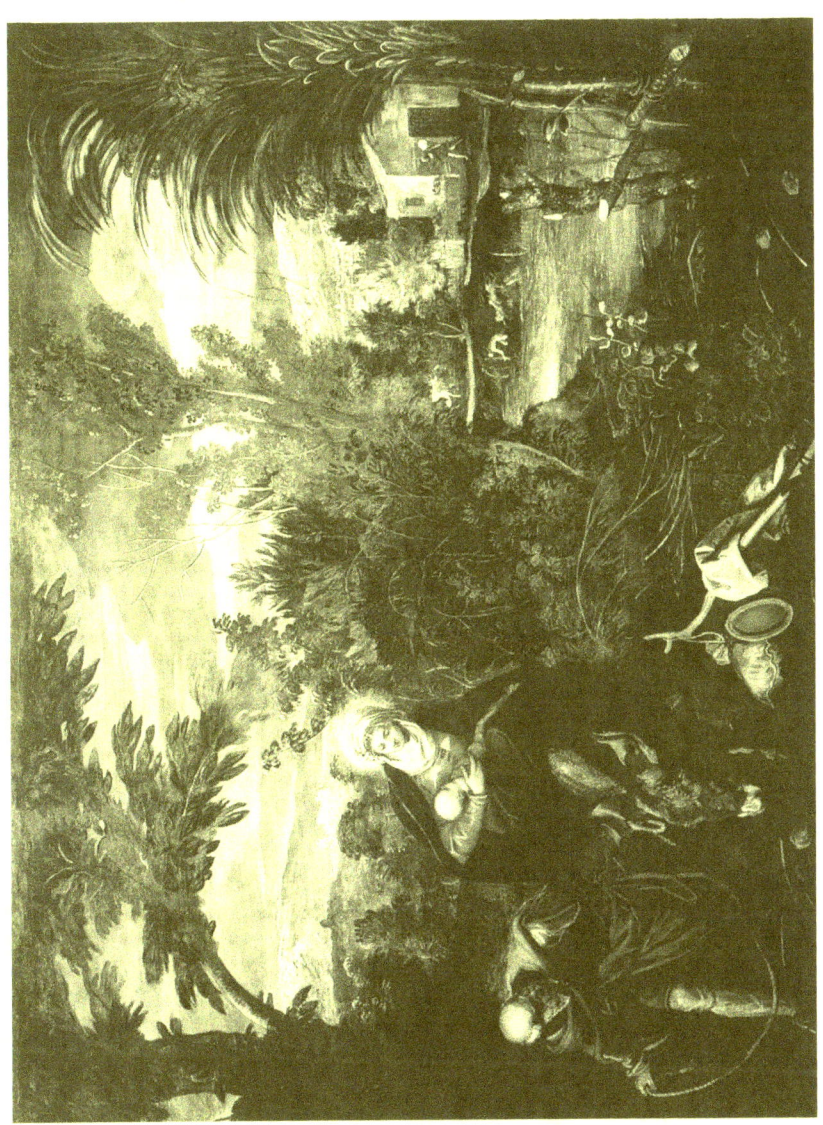

FIGURE NO. 38 ✦ Tintoretto, *Flight into Egypt*, 1582–7

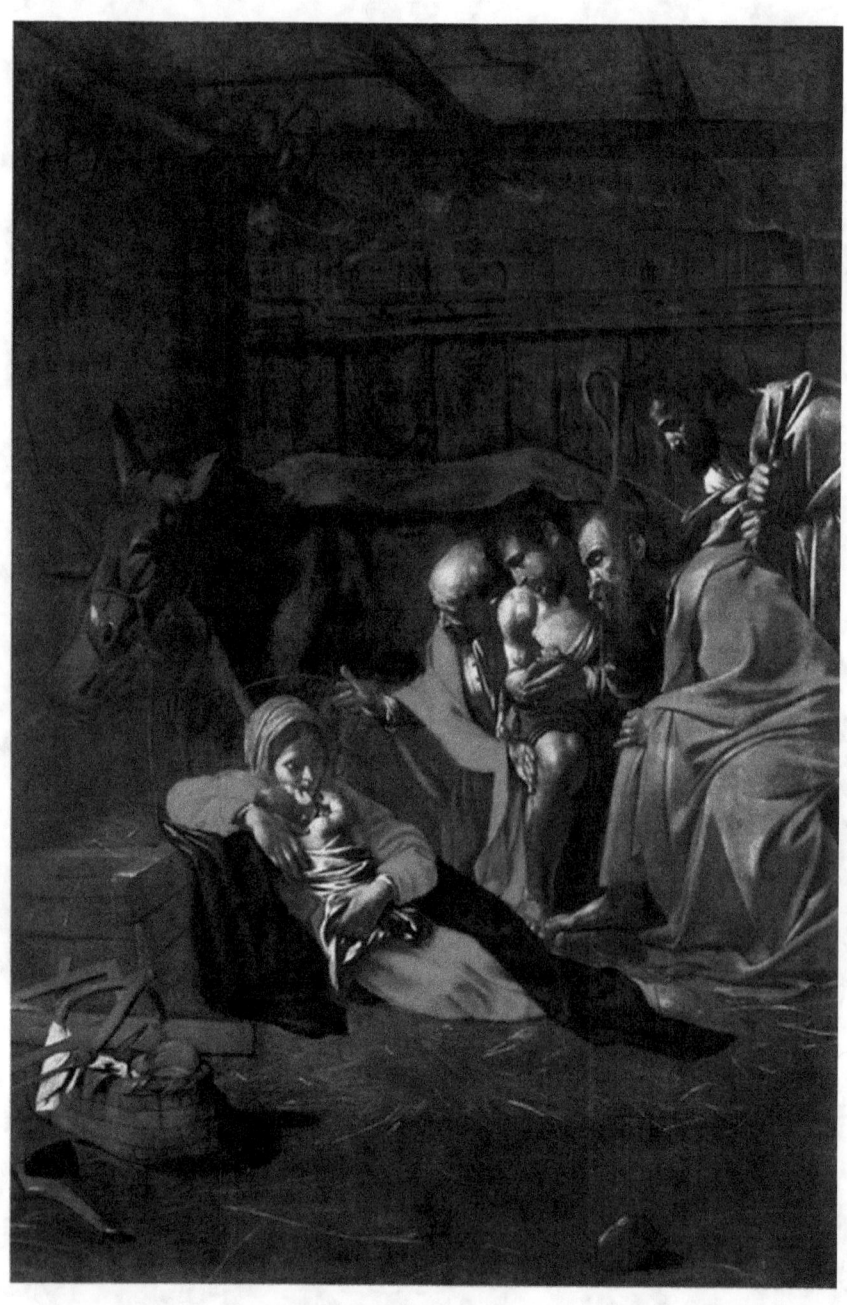

FIGURE NO. 39 ✠ Caravaggio, *Adoration of the Shepherds*, 1609

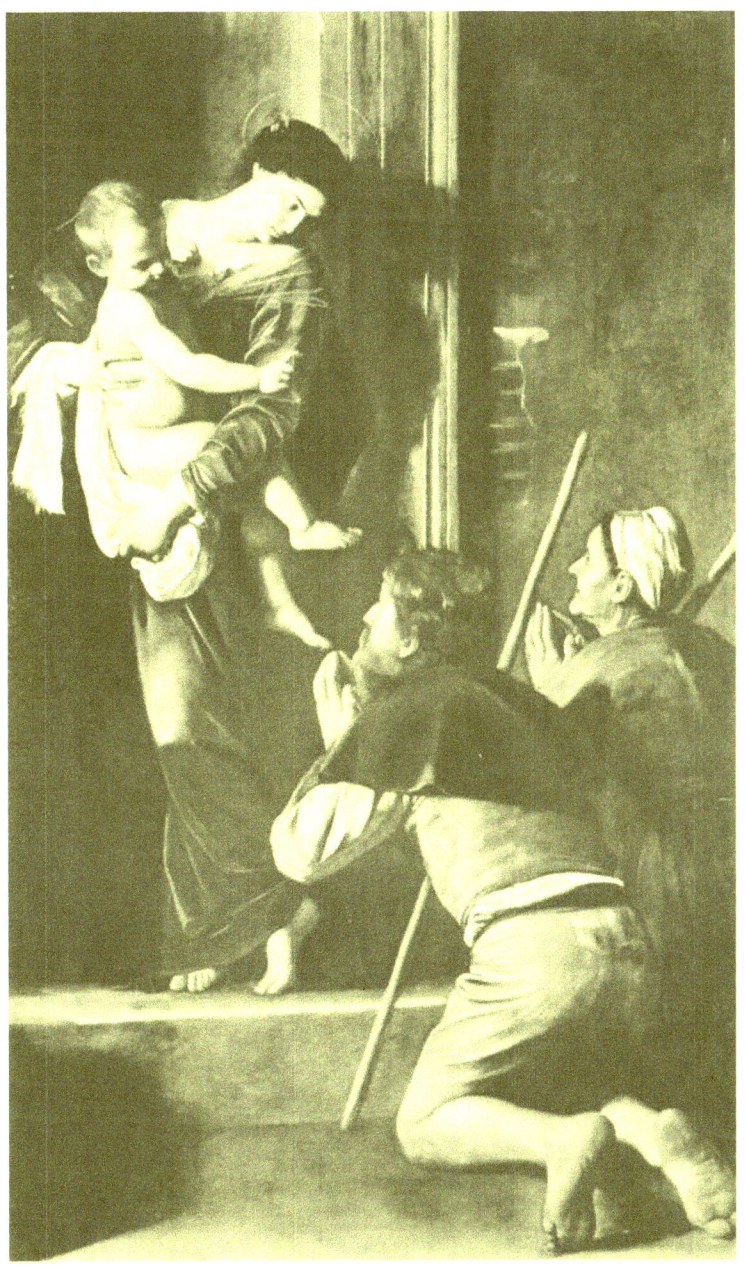

FIGURE NO. 40 ✦ Caravaggio, *Madonna of Loreto, c.* 1604

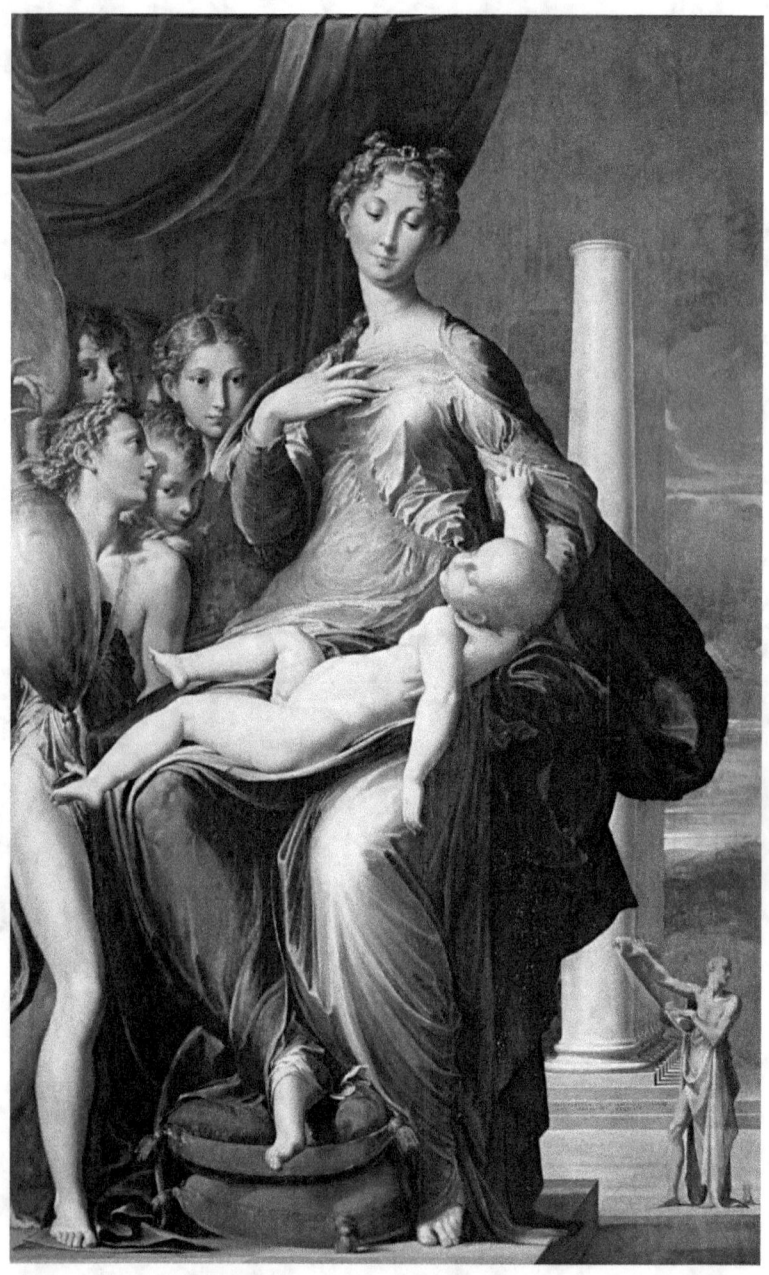

FIGURE NO. 41 ✦ Parmigianino, *Madonna of the Long Neck*, 1535–40

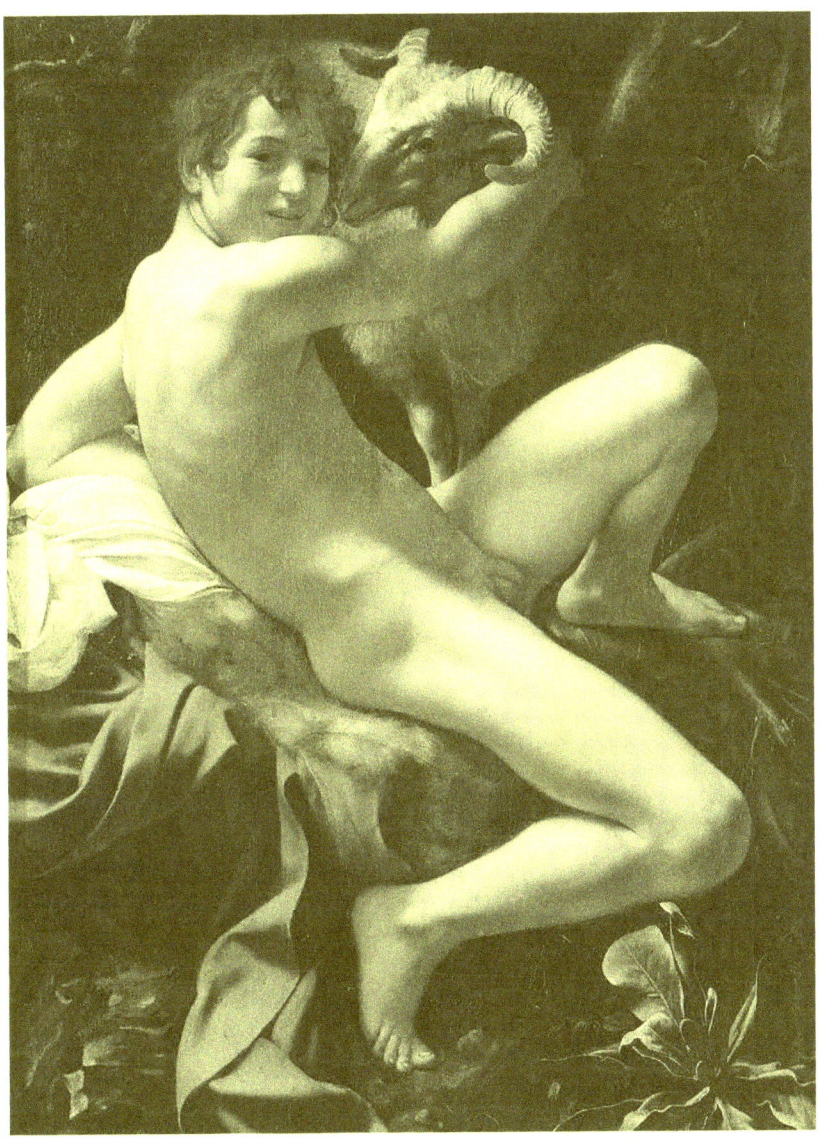

FIGURE NO. 42 ✦ Caravaggio, *Saint John the Baptist*, 1604

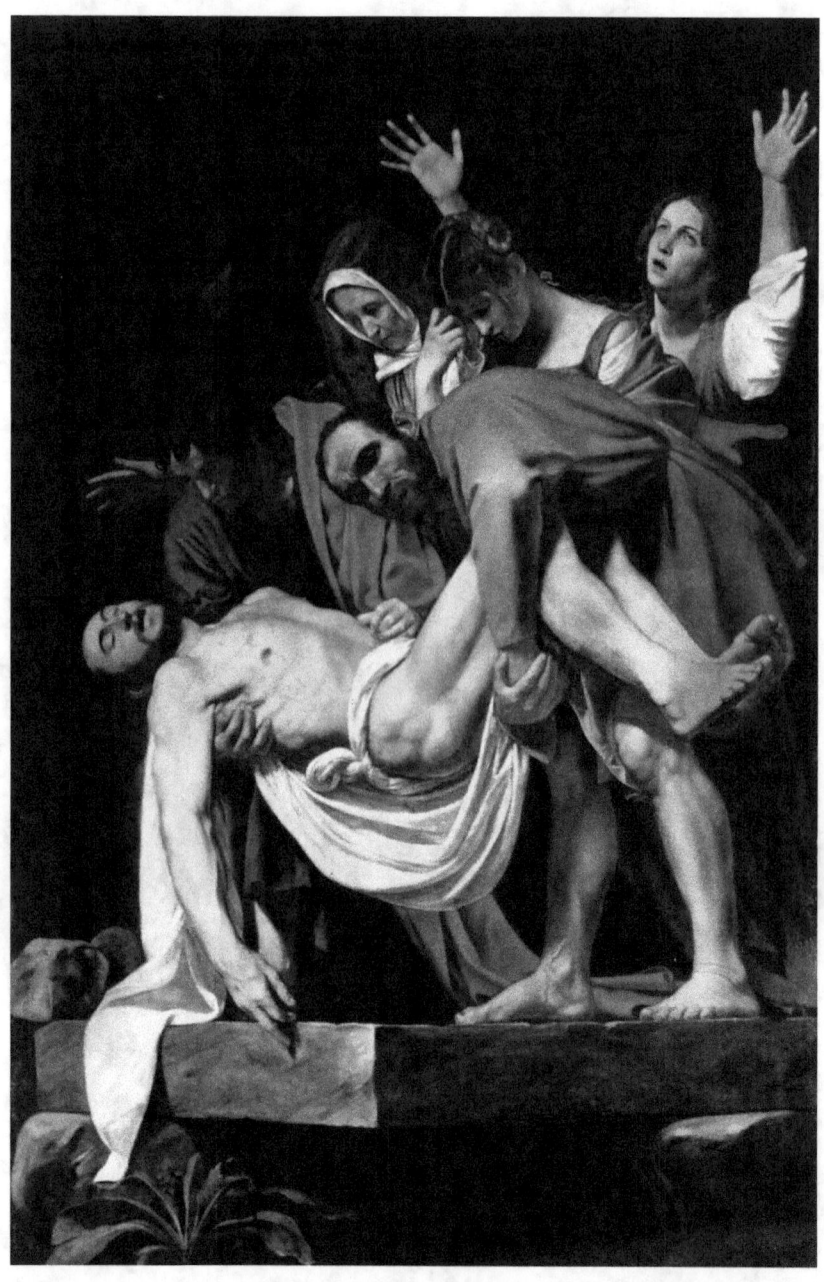

FIGURE NO. 43 ✛ Caravaggio, *Entombment, c.* 1603

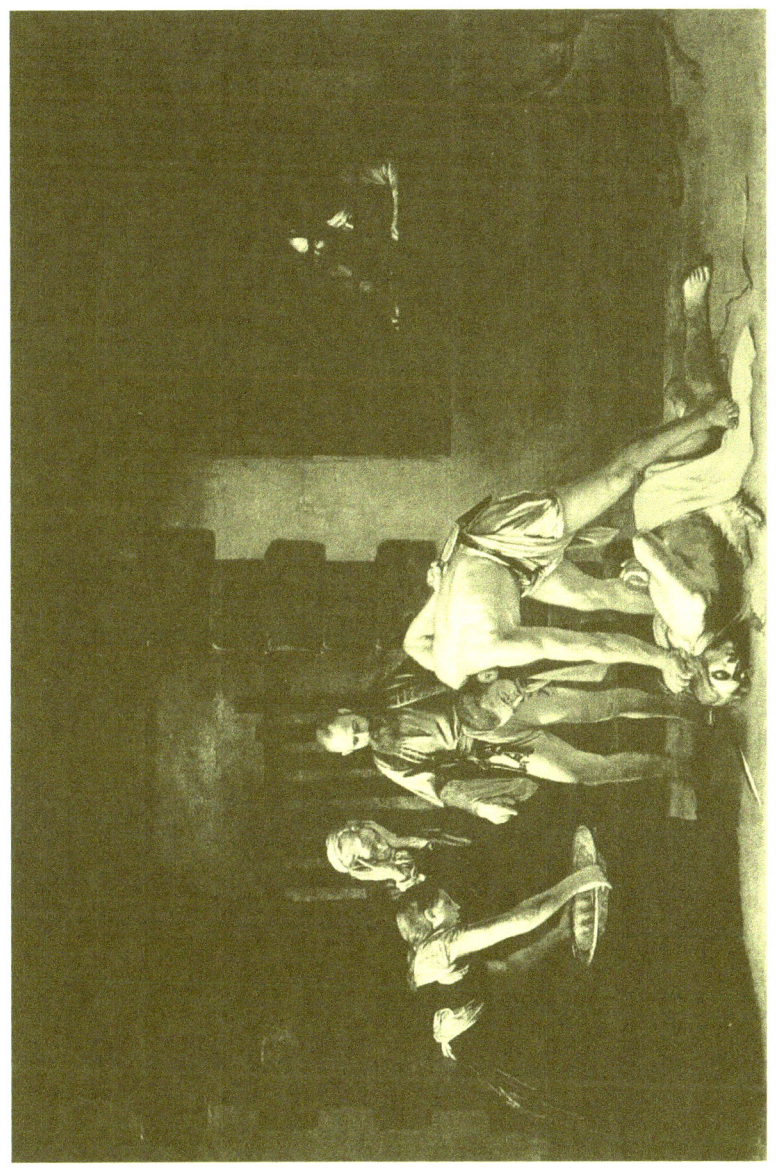

FIGURE NO. 44 ✣ Caravaggio, *Beheading of Saint John the Baptist*, 1608

www.ingramcontent.com/pod-product-compliance
Lightning Source LLC
Chambersburg PA
CBHW052317220526
45472CB00001B/163